Catholicism Under the Searchlight
of the Scriptures

Catholicism Under the Searchlight of the Scriptures

By
Evangelist John Carrara, Th. M., D.D.

By the same author,

"I Become an Evangelist"
"The Greatest Kidnapping Event About to Take Place"
"God's Searchlight"
"Modern Dangers"
"Why a Preacher and Not a Priest" (Biography)
"Enemies of Youth"

SECOND EDITION

ZONDERVAN

ZONDERVAN PUBLISHING HOUSE
Grand Rapids, Michigan

COPYRIGHT, MCMXLIII
ZONDERVAN PUBLISHING HOUSE

EIGHT FORTY-SEVEN N. OTTAWA AVENUE
GRAND RAPIDS, MICHIGAN

TO
DR. AND MRS. EDWARD ARMSTRONG
OF
PALISADE PARK, NEW JERSEY
UNDER WHOSE MINISTRY, AS
A CHRISTIAN LAYMAN, I
CAME TO KNOW
CHRIST
AS MY PERSONAL SAVIOUR,
THIS VOLUME IS
AFFECTIONATELY DEDICATED

ACKNOWLEDGMENT

THIS book on the subject of *Catholicism Under the Searchlight of the Scriptures,* formerly entitled *Out of the Wilderness,* is not written for the sake of saying sensational things. It is not written to make light or sport of anyone's religious belief. It is assumed that the great mass of people who follow any religious belief are honest and sincere in that belief. What is said, therefore, is said in all earnestness because the writer feels it his duty as a Christian minister. This book is not written with the hope of changing any large number of Roman or Greek Catholic adherents, or of leading them to give up their doctrines. There is little or no hope of that; however, there is sincere desire and prayer for the enlightenment of some who may be searching for the truth.

Most Catholics are discouraged from reading or hearing anything that in any way reflects upon or argues against their belief—and are afraid to do so. They are taught that all such books or articles or addresses are the result of blind prejudice and bias or else of misunderstanding of the doctrine. The large majority of Catholics do not examine for themselves the underlying conceptions of Roman Catholicism, and they are not willing to consider or weigh the force of any statement or argument made by those who have examined the doctrine in the light of God's Holy Word, especially if that statement or argument in any way seems to oppose Catholicism.

This book is the sincere product of one who has sat under the teachings of Catholicism, was confirmed in the Catholic Church and schooled in its teachings. It is written for three reasons: first, because it is believed that there are a great many people who are more or less inclined toward Catholicism but do not really know what Catholicism is in its fundamental teachings, nor what the logical and necessary outcome of such teachings must be in the lives of those who believe and follow them. In the

11

second place, this book is written with the hope of leading some of the Christian ministers, who may not have done so before, to see that it is their duty, in every way possible, to enlighten, in love, (not intolerance) their people as to the actual nature, teaching and necessary outcome of this fast-growing religious movement, before the whole of Christian America shall be engulfed after Catholicism has secured its hold upon the vast majority of the ignorant. Thirdly, from time to time, letters and pleadings from conscientious pastors have come, requesting a handbook to place in the hands of the Christian reading public which would reveal to them the teachings of Catholicism in the light of the Word of God. These pleadings have come to the author, who was for sixteen years a Roman Catholic and a student of Catholic teachings. Thus comes this sane, loving, understanding message on the paramount doctrines of Catholicism.

The author realizes that many other books and pamphlets have been written on this subject. He has hesitated in adding another volume to this list. However, after examining a large number of these books and pamphlets, not any have been found which seem to set forth the fundamental religious belief of Roman Catholicism and its necessary and actual outcome in the lives of those who accept it, in a full, systematic, yet simple way, and with sufficient page and line quotations from the acknowledged textbook of Catholicism to carry conviction to the mind of the ordinary reader. It was the recognition of the imperative need for such a work that led to the writing of this book.

The author appreciates beyond words the response, exceeding all expectations, which was given to the first edition.

I am indebted to Everett Pippen of Decatur, Illinois, for the drawing of the jacket.

Lake Mohawk, New Jersey   J. C.

CONTENTS

CONTENTS

Catholicism Under the Searchlight of the Scriptures

CHAPTER I

THE TRUE CHURCH

Now therefore ye are no more strangers and foreigners, but fellowcitizens with the saints, and of the household of God; and are built upon the foundation of the apostles and prophets, JESUS CHRIST HIMSELF being the chief corner stone; in whom all the building fitly framed together groweth unto an holy temple in the Lord: in whom ye also are builded together for an habitation of God through the Spirit.

—EPH. 2:19-22

There is one body, and one Spirit, even as ye are called in one hope of your calling.

—EPH. 4:4

FAILURE to recognize the distinctive character and heavenly calling of the true Church is responsible for a great deal of confusion in the world today among Christian people. Who knows what is meant by the true Church? There are so many divisions, so many cults today in Christianity and so many isms flourishing, that the world hardly knows what to believe. Even Christians themselves are puzzled concerning the real meaning of the term *true Church*. Until they get a vision of what God's Church means and what its supreme mission is, Christians do very little in regard to God's work.

The Church is not in the Old Testament. Christ says in Matt. 16:18, "Upon this rock I will build my church." He is telling the disciples that He *will build*, not, *I am building*. He reveals this great truth to them, which had never before been revealed. He is not the Messiah here of the Old Testament; He had been rejected and death was staring Him in the face. He told them things here that had been secret from the foundation of the world (13:35).

Before He started to build His Church He brought out the Jewish believers from the Jewish fold when He said, "Other sheep have I which are not of this fold." He would bring them, and then there would be one Shepherd and one flock. When the Church took form in the story in Acts, what took place? Did not the Jewish believers and the Gentile believers unite and form the Church?

In Christ's prayer in John 17 He showed Himself the great High Priest of the Church and told about this sweet, intimate unity with the Father and the Son that the believers were to have. "Neither pray I for these alone, but for them also which shall believe on me through their word; that they all may be one." Was not this a new revelation to both Gentile and Jew? Search the Old Testament and see if you can find anything like this. Christ did not say that He prayed for the saints of all ages—only for the believers who in the future would believe on Him through the ministry of the beginners.

The Church Age began with this union of Jew and Gentile described in the Acts; it continues today and will continue until the Lord comes. The Old Testament saints have their place in God's plan, but this new unity was the Church—Christ's body.

We all know the Church was started at Pentecost by the baptism of believers into one body in the Holy Spirit. This is the great truth of this dispensation—the dispensation of grace and the work of the Holy Spirit. Spirits were not baptized into the body of Christ, but the Apostles bear record of John's prophesying that Christ should baptize in the Holy Spirit. In John 1:32-34 we read: "And John bare record, saying, I saw the Spirit descending from heaven like a dove, and it abode upon him. And I knew him not: but he that sent me to baptize with water, the same said unto me, Upon whom thou shalt see the Spirit descending, and remaining on him, the same is he which baptizeth with the Holy Ghost. And I saw, and bare record that this is the Son of God." So Christ is the Baptizer.

In I Cor. 12:13 Paul says: "For by one Spirit are we all baptized into one body, whether we be Jews or Gentiles, whether we be bond or free; and have all been made to drink into one Spirit." The beginning of the baptism is the beginning of the body. We are baptized by the Lord Jesus in the Spirit. The only way into the body is the baptism in the spirit. The body, or Church, began on the day the baptism in the Spirit began.

Acts 1:5: "For John truly baptized with water; but ye shall be baptized with the Holy Ghost not many days hence," is a prediction that Pentecost would happen. In Acts 2 we have the fulfillment of the promise.

Acts 11:15, 16: "And as I began to speak, the Holy Ghost fell on them, as on us at the beginning. Then remembered I the word of the Lord, how that he said, John indeed baptized with water; but ye shall be baptized with the Holy Ghost." Peter calls the baptism in the Spirit the beginning, pointing back to Pentecost.

The day of Pentecost was the birthday of the church —Acts 2:47. After believers had been formed into one body, the Lord added to that body. Let us go to Ephesians for the revelation of the mystery of the church (Eph. 3:5). "Is now revealed unto his holy apostles and prophets by the Spirit." This revelation was a common possession of all the early church.

The church was one body—the body of Christ. Our Lord spoke of building it when He was here. Eph. 2: 19-22: "Now therefore ye are no more strangers and foreigners, but fellowcitizens with the saints, and of the household of God; and are built upon the foundation of the apostles and prophets, Jesus Christ himself being the chief corner stone; in whom all the building fitly framed together groweth unto an holy temple in the Lord: in whom ye also are builded together for an habitation of God through the Spirit."

In Matt. 16:18 we have the Church comprising all believers in this dispensation. This Church was responsible here on earth and had authority to discipline. Israel was completely set aside for the present age—Matt. 23:38. Paul says that all believers of this age are members of *one body*. Rom. 12:4-5: "For as we have many members in one body, and all members have not the same office: so we, being many, are one body in Christ, and every one members one of another."

I Cor. 12:20: "But now are they many members, yet but one body."

Col. 3:15: "And let the peace of God rule in your hearts, to the which also ye are called in one body: and be ye thankful."

Eph. 4:4: "There is one body, and one Spirit, even as ye are called in one hope of your calling."

This one body is the Church.

Let us look at the place of the Church in the plan of redemption. Paul, in Col. 1:24, touches upon the church: "That which is behind of the afflictions of Christ in my flesh for his body's sake, which is the church." Of this Church he was made a minister according to a stewardship given him for the Gentiles by God—fully to preach the Word of God. This meant the revelation of that "mystery which had been hid from all ages and generations, but now is made manifest to the saints." And that mystery—what is it? It is the indwelling of Christ in His believing people. This does not mean His indwelling in the believer as an individual merely, but His indwelling in the Church, His mystical body, of which every individual believer is a member by faith.

Here it is again in Eph. 3:3-9: "That the Gentiles should be fellowheirs, and of the same body, and partakers of his promise in Christ by the gospel" (6).

Let us review a little. After the world rejected God at Babel (Genesis 11) God chose Israel as the nation to be His witness to the world and to work out His original promise of redemption: (Gen. 13:15) "For all the land which thou seest, to thee will I give it, and to thy seed for ever."

And now after the world and Israel had rejected Him in the person of His Son, Jesus Christ, He chose the Church, which is called the body of Christ (Eph. 1:22-23), to be His witness and His instrument in this age for the execution of His promise. The Church did not come into being until after the death, resurrection and ascension of Jesus Christ: "And hath put all things under his feet, and gave him to be the head over all things to the church, which is his body, the fulness of him that filleth all in all" (Eph. 1:22-23). Its birthday was Pentecost.

Then let us answer the question: "Who founded the Christian Church?" Jesus Christ, on the fiftieth day after His resurrection, by the outpouring of the Holy Spirit, founded the Christian Church. The disciples then were endued with power to go forth (Matt. 16:18; Acts 2:1-11; I Cor. 3:11; Eph. 2:20).

After that, regular assemblies under direction of the Apostles were formed, the worship arranged, the Supper of the Lord administered. The outpouring of the Spirit was then necessary to the forming of the Church into the body of Christ. Christ said on the night of His betrayal to His disciples that the Holy Spirit would be *in* them. "For he dwelleth with you, and shall be *in* you" (John 14:17). Then when He went away He commanded them to remain in Jeruslaem until they should be baptized (Acts 1:4-5). They were then filled with the Holy Spirit and He came to dwell *in* them (Acts 2:1-4). Paul, in I

Cor. 12:12-13, speaks of believers as being one body with Christ and says that we were baptized into this body by one Spirit.

"He that is joined unto the Lord is one spirit" (I Cor. 6:17). We all know the story of Pentecost. The believers were all assembled in one mind in one place ready to be incorporated into Christ, the Head. He, being on high, sent down His Spirit to dwell in every one of them, making them all one. Since He dwells alike in every believer, He unites them to the Head, and so they are united one to another in the Head, Christ. Thus the body is formed.

This body of Christ has a certain work to do on the earth. In Eph. 4:1-16 we have that work outlined. We shall touch on it here and elaborate on it later. The gifts are spoken of, which the Head of the body bestows upon the believers. There are apostles, prophets, evangelists, pastors and teachers (verse 11). What is the reason for all this? The answer in verse twelve is "the perfecting of the saints, for the work of the ministry, for the edifying of the body of Christ." Then the apostles, prophets, evangelists, pastors and teachers—gifts to the Church— are not in themselves an end, but a means to an end.

Their purpose, as I have studied it, is to equip the whole body to engage in Christian ministry, each according to his ability or talent, the object being to build up of the body of Christ and to complete it as an organism, "Till we all come in the unity of the faith, and of the knowledge of the Son of God, unto a perfect man, unto the measure of the stature of the fulness of Christ" (vs. 13). This means the man—head and body. When that mystical organism is complete, when God has called out from among the nations all whom He intends in order to form the Church, then Christ and His body will have attained "the measure of the stature" of His fulness.

Let us pause to comment that the Church and the kingdom are not the same. When this body of Christ is com-

pleted and caught up to meet the Lord in the air (I Thess.
4:16-18), then Christ will return to the earth and in Him
will set up His kingdom promised to David. This kingdom will not come by persuasion through the preaching
of the gospel and the progress of Christianity, but through
divine power at the Second Advent of Christ (Ps. 2; Isa.
9:7; Dan. 2:35, 44-45; Zech. 14:1-9; Rev. 19:11-16).

The kingdom of heaven will merge into the kingdom
of God when Christ shall have delivered up the kingdom
to God, even the Father (I Cor. 15:24-28).

The church, *ecclesia,* means the "called-out ones" (Acts
2:47; Eph. 1:22-23; Heb. 12:23). What does "called-out
ones" mean? God, by His Holy Spirit, has called them
out of the world unto Himself through the exercise of
their faith in Christ (Col. 1:13).

The Church is not revealed in the plan of God until we
reach the New Testament. Christ is the seed of the
woman promised in Eden; the seed of Abraham and the
seed of David; the Son who should proceed out of Him
and in whom His kingdom should be established forever
(II Sam. 7:12-13).

When Christ appeared on the earth, He said, "The
kingdom of heaven is at hand." When Christ was rejected, He announced the new program about the Church
that had been kept secret (Rom. 16:25). He said, "Upon
this rock I will build my church; and the gates of hell
shall not prevail against it" (Matt. 16:18). This building
process, which began at Pentecost, is in progress until the
Church will be caught up to meet its Head in the air (I
Thess. 4:16-18).

The Church is built up and the kingdom is set up. The
Church has its elders and messengers and servants. The
kingdom has its heirs. We see, we receive, we enter, we
inherit the kingdom, but these terms are not used of our
relationship to the Church. The kingdom is advanced
and extended, but the Church is cleansed and edified.

The kingdom is a unit; the Church a body. The Church will reign with Christ; the kingdom will be reigned over by Christ and His Church. The Church is an election taken out of all nations; the kingdom will be universal. The Church is now in the world and longs for the time of deliverance, but the kingdom is still in the future: "Thy kingdom come. Thy will be done in earth, as it is in heaven." The Church is temporal: the kingdom is everlasting. Instead of the relation being one of mere covenant, it is one of birth. Instead of obedience bringing the reward of earthly greatness and wealth, the Church is taught to be content with food and raiment; to expect persecution and hatred; and it is seen that as distinctly as Israel stands connected with earthly and temporal things, so distinctly does the Church stand connected with spiritual and heavenly things.

In this dispensation neither Jew nor Gentile can be *saved* otherwise than by the exercise of that faith in the Lord Jesus Christ whereby both are "born again" (John 3:3, 16) and baptized into that "one body" (I Cor. 12:13) which is the Church (Eph. 1:22-23). In the Church the distinction of Jew and Gentile disappears. The rules of conduct given for Jew and Gentile are different. Contrast these Scriptures:

Deut. 7:1-2	Matt. 5:44
Exod. 21:24-25	I Cor. 4:12-13
	Matt. 5:39
Deut. 21:18-21	Luke 15:20-23

Even worship is contrasted. Israel could worship in but one place and at a distance from God, only approaching Him through a priest. The Church worships where two or three are gathered together, has boldness to enter into the holiest place and is composed of priests. Let us look at the following Scriptures: Lev. 17:8-9; Luke 1:10; Num. 3:10; Matt. 18:20; Heb. 10:19-20; I Pet. 2:5.

And in predictions concerning the future of Israel and the Church, the distinction is still more startling. The Church will be taken away from the earth entirely; restored Israel will have her great earthly splendor and power.

For the Church, these Scriptures need to be studied:

John 14:2-3	I Thess. 4:15-17
Phil. 3:20-21	John 3:2
Rev. 19:7-9	Rev. 20:6

For Israel we find these Scriptures:

Luke 1:31-33	Acts 15:14-16	Rom. 11:1, 11, 24-26
Isa. 11:11-12	Isa. 14:1	Jer. 16:14-15
Jer. 23:5-6	Jer. 32:37-38	Zeph. 3:14-15

It may be said that the Judaizing of the Church has done more than anything else to hinder her progress, pervert her mission and destroy her spiritually. Instead of pursuing her path laid out for her, of separation and hence persecution, world-hatred, poverty and non-resistance, she has lowered her purpose to civilizing the world and acquiring wealth, to the use of very imposing ritual, the building of grand churches and the division of the people into clergy and laity.

So we see that the kingdom is none of the Church's concern. The leaders of the Church should not be concerned in the business of "bringing in the kingdom." It is not until we come to the Epistles, which deal with the Church, that the goal of eternal life becomes heaven above. Israel was and is yet to be God's earthly people to whom and through whom the kingdom is promised.

Peter had no idea that the Gentiles were to unite with the Jews in the benefits of Christ's death because it required a special act of divine preparation to secure Peter's participation in ministering to Cornelius. Even then the Apostles made Peter account for what he had done. So we find the first church councils inquiring into granting Gentiles equal privileges with the Jews in the salvation wrought by our Saviour on the cross. James, as head or moderator of the council, tells how God visited the Gentiles to take out of them a people to bear His name: Christian.

Acts 15:14-16 says: "Simeon hath declared how God at the first did visit the Gentiles, to take out of them a people for his name. And to this agree the words of the prophets; as it is written, After this I will return, and will build again the tabernacle of David, which is fallen down; and I will build again the ruins thereof, and I will set it up." So we see that the kingdom is not the concern of the Church. The kingdom will be reëstablished after the Messiah's return when the Church is complete, has finished her mission on earth and has been taken up.

Jesus made it plain that the coming of the kingdom did not concern the Apostles or the Church. The Church's work will be finished before the kingdom begins. God ceased to stand sponsor for the Jewish nation when the Temple veil was rent from the top to the bottom and the Shechinah glory was withdrawn from the Temple. Then it was that God ceased to stand sponsor for the nation. Then the Kingdom of Promise was postponed. This continues throughout the Church Age. Then when the Church is raptured out of the world, Christ will return and reëstablish the kingdom.

Let us summarize our findings: The Church is not to be confounded with the kingdom. The Church is compared to a house (I Tim. 3:15), to a temple (I Cor. 3:16-17), to a body (I Cor. 12:27-31), but never to a kingdom. Christ is the Head of His Church (Eph. 1:22, 4:15; Col. 1:18). The Church is a mystery and was revealed to Paul (Eph. 3:1-11). The mystery was that God was going to form an entirely new thing composed of both "Jew and Gentile," to be called the Church.

The purpose of God in this dispensation is seen in the divine program outlined by James in his address to the first church council held in Jerusalem (Acts 15: 13-15) when he declared that God had visited the Gentiles to take out of them a people for His name.

It is not God's program to bring the kingdom or to set up the kingdom in this dispensation or to convert the world, but the gathering out of an elect body, the Church. The church is a "called-out body"; it is the body of Christ. In Eph. 1:22-23 we read: "And hath put all things under his feet, and gave him [Jesus] to be the head over all things to the church, which is his body, the fulness of him that filleth all in all." The context shows (verse 20) that this headship was not possible until Jesus had been raised from the dead and seated at the right hand of God.

The Church then, we see, did not exist until Christ became the Head. The Church, then, is the body of which Christ is the Head. In I Cor. 12:12-13 we are told how this body is formed: "For as the body is one, and hath many members, and all the members of that one body, being many, are one body: so also is Christ. For by one Spirit are we all baptized into one body, whether we be Jews or Gentiles, whether we be bond or free; and have been all made to drink into one Spirit." From this we see that it is the baptism of the Spirit that incorporates us into the body of Christ—that is, there could be no Church until the Day of Pentecost. Larkin, in *Rightly Dividing the Word,* agrees with this.

The fact remains clear that the Church is a "body" made up of "living members." It is not an organization, as the Roman Catholic Church claims, but an *organism.* As the human body is for the manifestation of a personality, so the Church, the body of Christ, is for the purpose of manifesting "His personality" (Larkin, *Rightly Dividing the Word*). We then see that the only way possible for the world to see the works of Christ is through His body, the Church (I Cor. 15:38).

The Church is not only the body of Christ; it is to be His bride. At present it is but a virgin espoused (II Cor. 11:2). Many hold that the Church cannot be both the body and the bride of Christ and that the bride must be Israel. But we must not overlook that there are two brides mentioned in the Scriptures—one we see clearly in the Old Testament and the other in the New Testament. The one in the Old Testament is Israel, the bride of Jehovah; the one in the New Testament is the Church, the bride of Christ. Of Israel it is said, "Thy Maker is thine husband" (Isa. 54:5). Because of her whoredoms, Israel is a cast-off wife, but Jehovah promises to take her back when she ceases from her adulteries (Jer. 3:1-18; Hos. 2:1-23, 3:1-5). She will not be taken back as a virgin but as a wife (Larkin in *Rightly Dividing the Word*). But it is a virgin that the Lamb (Jesus Christ) is to marry; so the wife of the Old Testament cannot be the bride of the New. The wife (Israel) is to reside in the earthly Jerusalem during the millennium, while the bride (the Church) will reside in the New Jerusalem, which comes down out of heaven. These distinctions make it clear that Israel cannot be the bride of Christ.

If the Church, as we know her, had her origin at Pentecost and will end at the Rapture of the saints (I Thess. 4:14-17), then only those who are saved between those events belong to the Church.

The mission of the Church, as we have seen, is not to be an *organization*, but to be an *organism*. She is not a social club nor a place of amusement nor a house of merchandise for sale of indulgences or the sale of commodities whereby the money of the ungodly can be secured to save the church-members a little self-sacrifice; nor is she a reform bureau. This is not the work of the Church. But the Church's work is to carry this gospel to the world.

"Evangelism," not social service or reform or education or legislation, will proclaim Christ's message to a lost and dying world. When the Church is completed at the close of this dispensation (grace), it is to be caught up at the Rapture, at Christ's coming in the air (I Thess. 4:13-17). After the Rapture, the Church will be judged, not for sin, but for works.

In Mark 16:15 we have the marching orders of the Church. As the Church in this age, let us listen to the words of the Head of the body. Let us gird ourselves and refresh ourselves and go forth to the fray!

There never was a greater need for the Church than there is today. The world is full of confusion and torn with strife. Unbelief is rampant. In such a world and in such an age we dare not falter or trifle or bicker over small matters, but we must reconsider the message of the Church and her method from the beginning. The Church is not to reform this world or to take part in the politics thereof. Her business alone is to give out the message; win converts to Jesus Christ; teach them the doctrines in the Word of God; and to graft them into the body of Christ, which is the Church. When man's heart is right, he will treat his neighbors right, and then politics can become Christian.

Let us return to the way of the Early Church when each day was a thrilling adventure; when the Church proclaimed her message and conquered a pagan world. First love and then duty, once again proclaiming the love of God—THIS IS THE SUPREME MISSION OF THE CHURCH.

The chief duty of the Church, I repeat, is to proclaim the gospel, for the *gospel* alone can change the human heart. No laws, no forced improvements, no planned economy, no regimentation can make the world happy and prosperous, unless man's heart is changed. Of course we should help suffering and improve social conditions. Christians will better social conditions, for when their hearts are changed, human nature takes an upward trend and man loves his neighbor as himself.

The Church is not here as a reform agency, but to preach the gospel so that politics may become Christian. The Early Church proclaimed her message and conquered a pagan world. Let us return to that first duty and make known God's love to a lost world. The urgency of this call of Christ constitutes the supreme mission of the Church. The gospel is the only power that transforms the heart of man. If a man's heart is right with God, outward conditions will make little difference. He will be content. The unregenerated heart of man is never satisfied.

The gospel is the chief duty of the Church. It gets at the foundation of all wrong and evil. The gospel alone, I repeat, can change the human heart. The material and earthly can never satisfy the soul of man. The soul does not belong to this world and at death departs to its own sphere. You cannot feed your soul on the husks of the world, for it hungers and thirsts after God and the things of God. How much of the Church's time, strength and money are spent in ministering earthly things to a heavenly soul!

Every attempt to attract people fails when we do this, but if we preach the gospel it has the power to attract men. Give them the bread and water of life, as they are hungry and thirsty for it. The glory is that when the soul is purified, redeemed and uplifted into heavenly places, it exalts the body. The body then becomes the temple of the Holy Spirit. We think of Paul's words in I Cor. 6:20: "For ye are bought with a price: therefore glorify God in your body, and in your spirit, which are God's."

If we minister only to the body, as is now done in totalitarian states and here in our own country, the body will drag down the soul to its own level and we shall have crime. When the Church turns from her work of preaching the gospel and engages in other enterprises, she is only one of many agencies doing good. But she is the only one appointed by Christ for this work of His. If she neglects her duty, the work goes undone, and the Word is not preached. We have been preaching the gospel in the heathen lands for a hundred years at least, and when we come home we find in our own land great sections destitute of His Word: no churches, no gospel, no spiritual blessings; towns without a meeting-place, and millions of young people growing up without the Church. There are twenty-two million children that do not go to Sunday school in the United States, someone has said. Our land is given over to lawlessness and crime; great cities are under the control of racketeers and gangsters, but the Church is richer today than she was one hundred years ago and could exert a mighty influence if she were Christ's "church of the firstborn." How can this be? The Church so called, has forgotten her gospel.

If every church and every professing Christian were only ready to obey this great commission of Christ as He intended, our land would not be godless, unhappy and lawless. Everyone sees that our moral and spiritual development has not kept pace with our material and mental development. It is dangerous to make men clever and skillful and not make them good at the same time. We have trained them to become great inventors and to make death-dealing rays and planes, but we have not taught them of the Christ to rule their spirits. Scientists have begun to see where these destructive creations have led us. Sir Oliver Lodge startled the world a year or so ago by saying that we know things that never should have been known and that we never dreamed that radio would be used to bomb women and children from the air. We never thought that civilians would be bombed behind the lines as the Spanish civilians have been. Dorothy Thompson says that although we made these dreadful engines of war, Christian nations at least limited and controlled their use, but we never thought about heathen nations who would not be restrained by love or pity. The Japanese were surprised that nations questioned their use for killing women and children. Had these implements not been created for use?

The Church has forgotten her gospel and neglected her task. The Great Commission is for the Church—it is her supreme mission. If the Church does not do it, the Word will not be preached, and the gospel will not be proclaimed.

In Christ's time, there were many gross political and social wrongs. Christ saw all this and He felt pity and love for the common people. His heart was broken as He beheld. His disciples were chosen not from the rich or literate but from the ranks of human workmen. But Christ never engaged in any reforms to force a change in these conditions. He never joined the revolutionaries to deliver the oppressed. He came down from heaven and lived to tell of His Father's love. He shed His blood for them that through His death men might be saved. And when He rose again and before He left, He told His disciples to go everywhere telling the good news. He knew that men would go everywhere with the gospel and if it found a lodging place that it would destroy injustice, right wrongs, drive away despair and implant love and a song in every heart.

Let us never think that the gospel needs to be pieced out with something else—some earth-made means—a social gospel that will reach men quicker. There is nothing quicker than the gospel. It is a two-edged sword, piercing man immediately and changing him in the twinkling of an eye. Let us not be led astray. The gospel embodies pity, brotherly love, sympathy, kindness, desire to help the helpless and suffering. We do not need any social gospel, but the plain unadulterated Word of God.

There is a question in many minds as to the meaning of "Holy Catholic Church" in the Apostles' Creed. Let us look at the meaning of the word "catholic," first historically, and then popularly. Historically it came into use during the Apostolic Era. The word merely signifies universal, or general. During the Apostolic Age and for some time the Church presented the appearance of one great brotherhood. This brotherhood had communion of saints. When false teachers came in, those true believers banded together to maintain the unity of the Church and soon called themselves Catholics. In order to preserve this unity, bishops were appointed. The rights of the bishop were given to him for the honor of the Church and not by divine right. When the Roman Bishop became the Bishop of Bishops, then the Roman Church became the principal church, and the unity of the priesthood arose.

The holy catholic Church does not mean to us what it does to the Roman Catholic Church. We do not accept the teaching of the Roman Catholic Church concerning the primacy of the bishop and the Church of Rome. It was not so in the Apostolic Church. There is nothing in the teachings of the New Testament to warrant it.

What is the popular meaning of the word "catholic"? Catholic means universal, or general. The Church of Christ is universal, one in an all pervading unity, which has always been preserved. The Scriptures teach that there is but one Church, which is called the body of Christ, of which He is the head and every believer a member: Rom. 12:5; I Cor. 12:12; Eph. 4:4.

Every Christian upon his acceptance of Christ as Saviour has by the Spirit of God been placed in the mystical body of Christ, the Church. Each believer is not only united by the Holy Spirit to the Head in heaven, but is also united to every other believer in earth in whom the Spirit of God dwells. This is the great truth of the oneness of the body. Christ is linked eternally with His own and "all are one in Christ Jesus" (Gal. 3:28.)

If there is one body of which every believer is a member and Christ the Head, we do not need other bodies with men at their head. No one can join the body of Christ any more than your finger can join your body. The believer is born again by the Spirit (I Cor. 6:17; Eph. 4:16; Col. 2:19). Christ should be sufficient as a Head. Each assembly, therefore, should have Christ as its Head. Believers are members, the Word of God the authority, the Holy Spirit its power and the glory of Christ the aim!

We are not told to make a unity, but to keep the unity of the Spirit. How much more powerful would be the testimony of the Church if there were unity! How much more effective would be the testimony of the whole Christian community if we would magnify our oneness in Christ rather than our denomination. We have heard it said that in the early times of the apostles there were congregations but no Congregationalists! baptized ones but no Baptists! There were presbyters but no Presbyterians! method in the Church but no Methodists! bishops but no Episcopalians! there men trembled at the Word, but no Quakers! They were CHRISTIANS, meeting in the name of the Lord, and obedient to His Word! This is true communion of saints. Then fellowship of all true Christians centered upon and was occupied wholly with the Lord. Christians are saints because they are centered in Christ. In their union with Him, they have communion. The Church, then, is the living or visible witness of the invisible Lord. It is a holy union only when it is the reincarnation of its Holy Lord. It is catholic only as it recognizes the universal priesthood of all believers. Each believer has the same standing in grace. The Church is the only Church when it holds fast to its Head and seeks to honor Him. The Church is a channel for communicating the living Christ to a world dead in trespasses and sins. Christ's impact upon the world through the members of His body, the Church, has changed the whole face of civilization. When He instituted His Church and endued it with the power of the Holy Spirit, with the fact of His incarnate Deity, His redeeming death, His mighty resurrection, His all-powerful gospel of redemption and His glory, the world was pagan. The whole of civilization was changed.

We need this spirit today. Philosophy, science, intellectualism, social gospel will not do. We need the *living Christ*. The Church must recognize the presence and power of her Lord and be true to Him, her Head. We need church honesty and integrity. We need faithfulness. We do not need a new interpretation for this age, but a new devotion to the Christ of the Ages. Christ is the only Head of the Church, I repeat. He is present with her all the time. The Church of this age must know He is with her if she is to keep her candlestick lighted. It is her only hope.

"I am the first and the last: I am he that liveth and was dead; and behold, I am alive forevermore, Amen; and have the keys of hell and death." When the Church recognizes and acts upon the fact of His immediate presence with her and that He is watching the glow of her candlesticks, then only can you feel a glow in saying: "I believe in the holy catholic Church; the communion of saints."

I want you to belong to the one true Church—the Church outside of which there is no salvation. Do you belong? Where is this one true Church? What is the nature of this one true Church? How may I know this Church? I want you to ask questions.

The one true Church is composed of all believers in the Lord Jesus—all God's elect—all converted men and women—all true Christians. In whomsoever we can discern the election of God the Father, the sprinkling and cleansing of the blood of God the Son, the sanctifying work of God the Spirit, we see a member of Christ's true Church. All in this Church are born again of the Spirit; they all possess repentance toward God, faith toward Christ and holiness of life and conversation; they all hate sin and love Christ. They worship differently in form but with one heart. They are all led by one Spirit; they have one foundation; they all love the inspired Word of God—the Bible—and are joined to one Head—the Christ.

Their life does not hang upon church membership or baptism or communion or forms of worship, but it depends upon the Head, the One Shepherd, the One Chief Bishop—Jesus Christ. He by His Spirit admits the members of this Church, though our ministers and evangelists show us the door. Until He opens the door, no man on earth can open it, and if He opens it, no man can shut it. Once let a man repent and believe the gospel, and that moment he becomes a member of that Church. He may not have the opportunity to be baptized with water, as my dear brother who was killed before he could be baptized, but he has the baptism of the Spirit which is better. He may not be allowed to partake of communion, but he eats Christ's body and drinks Christ's blood by faith every day, and none can prevent him. He might even be excommunicated by ordained men and cut off from the professing church, but all that cannot shut him out of the true Church.

This Church does not depend on forms and ceremonies, big cathedrals, pulpits, fonts, vestments, organs and marble altars; nor does its money come from rich and influential citizens. No endowments, no king, no government keeps this Church. It lives on when driven into the wilderness, into dens and caves of the earth—even by its friends. It needs nothing but Christ and His Spirit, and so it cannot die.

"What titles does this Church have in Scripture?" you ask. We know it is the body of Christ. Then go to your Bible. There the Church is called the flock, the household of faith, the family of God, God's building, God's foundation and God's temple of the Holy Ghost.

Furthermore, it is the "church of the firstborn whose names are written in heaven"; a royal priesthood, a peculiar people, a chosen generation, a purchased possession, the habitation of God, the salt of the earth; the wheat of the earth; the light of the world; *this* is the holy catholic Church: this is that Church to which the Lord Jesus promises, "The gates of hell shall not prevail against it" (Matt. 16:18). And He promises in Matt. 28:20, "I am with you alway, even unto the end of the world."

Here is the Church that has unity. All the members are taught by one Spirit. They agree about the Trinity— God, Christ and the Holy Spirit. They know they were sinners and have faith, repentance, and have been washed in the blood. Those in this Church know they must live holy lives through Christ, and they love their Bibles and prayer. They are all looking for His coming, and are all of one mind on these things.

These members are not holy by profession, but holy in name and in act, deed and reality, in life and truth. They are conformed to the image of the Christ. No unholy one belongs to this church, for each member is united to Christ and therefore cannot be unholy.

This is the only Church truly catholic. It is universal. Its members are found in every part of the world where the gospel is received and believed. This Church consists of men of every tribe and nation and a countless number of every name and tongue! But all are one in Christ Jesus!

"But if I tarry long, that thou mayest know how thou oughtest to behave thyself in the house of God, which is the church of the living God, the pillar and ground of the truth" (I Tim. 3:15). The Catholic Church has used this text for the assertion that the church is an *organization* instead of an *organism*.

In this text the phrase "the house of God" does not refer to a meeting place called a "church." The New Testament never used the word in that sense. The "house of God" is a building made up of true believers, as we have it in Eph. 2:21. The house of God consists of God's born-again people wherever they may be. Every believer is at all times in the house of God.

This house of God is called the Church of the living God. It is the living God's Church for it is built of Him, inhabited by Him and completed through Him.

This is the same church that is elsewhere in Scripture called the body of Christ. Christ and the Church form an organism, just as the physical body is an organism. Neither Christ nor the Church is complete without the other. No closer identification could possibly be expressed, or even conceived, than that declared in I Cor. 12:12: "For as the body is one, and hath many members, and all the members of that one body, being many, are one body: so also is Christ." Had we been writing that, undoubtedly we would have stated, "so also is the Church," but the Spirit put it, "so also is Christ," identifying both Head and body under that one name.

Loyalty to the Church, then, does not necessarily mean loyalty to an organization, but to the organism, the body itself. By loyalty we mean true allegiance, faithful devotion. To be loyal is to be constant and faithful in any relationship implying trust and confidence.

The body is, however, represented on earth in the various local assemblies. There is no limit to the assemblies, but there is but one body. Every true assembly is gathered on one ground—that of one body, or one organism.

It is proper to distinguish between the assembly and the organism. We think, however, that sometimes the distinction is over-emphasized. We believe that Scripture identifies the assembly with the organism. For example, Ephesians declares to us the truth concerning the body of Christ, but makes very little distinction between the body and the assembly to which the epistle is addressed.

"The fact of the assembly is quite clear in Scripture, and the value is beyond question. The true assembly is something peculiar; it is unique; it is unlike any other gathering."

IT DOES MATTER with which local assembly we are identified. Some say, "Well, I don't think it makes much difference with which local body one is identified, for they are all aiming at the same place anyway." Did you ever miss anything at which you aimed? A friend of mine told about never hitting the mark in target practice. He learned afterward that he had shut the wrong eye. Sometimes when people shoot they shut both eyes. There are a great many so-called assemblies of God that shut both eyes and never hit the truth.

There is an ever-increasing disposition to multiply sects and exalt human heads. If it be a matter of pleasing ourselves, we have a variety of man-made assemblies from which to choose. If we aim to please God, we must identify ourselves with that assembly which truly represents the body of Christ. All human organizations exalt man and eventually centralize thought, attention and power in man.

We talk too much about being a member of A church. True believers are members of THE Church. A member of the Church should be identified with a local assembly.

We are told in Scripture to keep the unity of the Spirit. This is a unity composed of many members—not a mere union of parts. The many members constitute one body.

This unity can be the result of the work of the Holy Spirit only, and can take place in Jesus Christ only. This unity we are told to keep. The only possible way it can be kept is by assembling in the Name of the Lord Jesus, and in His Name only. There is only one Name which God has honored above every other name—the Name of the Lord Jesus. That is the Name which the devil hates above every other name; therefore the devil uses all his influence and power to keep us from gathering in His Name. How he must chuckle over some of our gatherings!

We can be gathered in the Name of the Lord Jesus only by the Holy Spirit. The Holy Spirit will gather us only in the Name of the Lord Jesus.

We have stated that the Church of the living God is the body of which Christ is the Head—the organism.

When Christ was on earth He functioned for God as His Representative. The Church is the only representative of Christ in the world. How important it is that the Church should not misrepresent Him!

Christ said, "He that hath seen me hath seen the Father." It should be true that "to see the Church is to see Christ." "He that saith that he abideth in him, ought also to walk even as he walked." "Put ye on, therefore, the Lord Jesus Christ."

Every true believer ought to be a sample of the Lord Jesus Christ. Christ dwells in every individual believer as well as in the corporate body. Yieldedness to Him will mean a reproduction of the Lord Jesus Christ. We certainly cannot be loyal to the Church if we misrepresent Christ. All the newspapers, placards, folders and posters that the printing press is able to publish cannot counteract one disloyal member of the Church. Neither can all the printed matter equal one good, consistent, faithful, loyal member.

The Church of the living God is the pillar and ground (foundation) of the truth. Note: Not A pillar and A foundation, as if there were others, but THE pillar and THE foundation of the truth. The Church is the only repository of redemption truth in the whole wide world.

A pillar supports the roof, but the pillar itself rests upon a foundation; so this is like saying, "The Church of the living God is the pillar, yea, more, even the *foundation* of the truth."

The Church is the pillar and foundation of the truth in the sense that it bears up, supports, displays the truth. It is the stay of the truth. It is God's instrument in the world for the continuance of the truth in the earth in the face of all opposition.

Mark this: The church that does not hold the truth is not a church—it is never recognized as such by God no matter what men may call it.

The expression "the pillar and the ground of the truth" does not mean that the truth rests upon the Church so that if the Church failed the truth would fail, but that the Church rests upon the truth so that if the truth be lost the Church will fail.

The Church is built on the foundation laid by Jesus Christ and holds His doctrines. It aims at Apostolic faith and Apostolic practice. No other church will endure unto the end. Nothing can overthrow or destroy it, and the gates of hell shall not prevail against it. It lives through fire and water. You may persecute, oppress, imprison, beat, behead and burn its members, but the true Church is never extinguished. "Truth crushed to earth will rise again." When crushed in one land, it springs up in another. Tyrants arise and slay, but they pass away and go to their own place. The true Church outlives them all and sees them buried. The true Church is an anvil that has broken many a hammer and will still continue to break them. The true Church is a burning bush that never consumes.

No member of this wonderful Church can perish. Once enrolled in or born into this Church, sinners are safe for eternity. They are never cast out. However, as Paul says, that does not give license to sin, but if we are in Christ we are righteous in His righteousness. God takes us in; Christ continually intercedes for us; daily we are renewed and sanctified by the power of the Holy Ghost. So He surrounds us. Not one bone of Christ's mystical body shall ever be broken. No one can pluck these sheep out of the Shepherd's hand.

This is the Church that does the work of Christ on earth. Few in numbers but mighty in power, it shakes the universe. Its members can change the fortunes of kingdoms by their prayers; they spread the knowledge of Christ far and wide. They are the lifeblood of any country. By their prayers to their God on high, they stay the hand of disaster. "Upon this rock [Himself, the Son of God] I will build my church and the gates of hell shall not prevail against it" (Matt. 16:18).

What is the work of this Church of Christ's? The Apostles regarded themselves as evangelists who were called to proclaim the glad and glorious tidings of God's amazing love in providing salvation for all mankind. They loved to tell of His atonement for sin, His death, His resurrection, His ascension into heaven and His coming again to judge the world and reign with His saints. The great commission of the Church of their day was to glorify God in the conversion of sinners. They had the joy of seeing a great company come into the Church, and then each of them became an evangelist to bring in more into the peace and joy of God's forgiveness. As the Early Church kept to this task of making disciples through its preaching, it became a great power during the first three centuries.

Look at the Church so called today! How she neglects this commission! The Early Church preached Jesus

Christ and Him crucified, but in our day the Church ignores Christ's atonement for sin. In modern preaching the gospel of works is substituted for the gospel of redeeming love and grace. We want not the fruits of the gospel but the gospel of grace, which leads to salvation and makes possible the fruits of the Spirit. Christian ethics will not save the world, as some ministers think. They make man his own power of God unto salvation.

The Church must preach the great evangelical doctrines —atonement, justification, regeneration, judgment, eternal life, eternal death and the coming again of the King, or she will cease to be His instrument on earth for the gathering-in of His body. No one belongs to this body of His unless he is born again, or regenerated. No longer are men and women warned of their danger in remaining out of Christ and asked to receive Him as their Saviour. There are thousands of churches today where real conversions are unknown.

In the earlier church of our time, the morning service was devoted to exhortation of believers and edification of believers and instruction in the art of soul-winning. The evening service was an evangelistic service for conversion of unbelievers. The one end in view was the salvation of the lost. The hymns, the Scripture, the preparation of the sermon, the prayer and expectancy of the congregation—all were influenced by the thought that it was the grand vocation of the Church to win souls for Christ! Christians made efforts to bring friends, neighbors, loved ones under the sound of the gospel. There was such a spirit of prayer and sympathy that the Holy Spirit could work with convicting and converting power. What joy among God's people when one soul accepted the Lord!

Where is that today? The evening service in some churches has lost this evangelistic enthusiasm and has become a service of worship. Then, since people went to church in the morning, they do not go in the evening; so the evening service in most churches is gone! Those who miss that evening service go to missions in the evening, for they love the simplicity of the evangelistic meetings. The mission service keeps the heart burning in love toward Christ and gives an opportunity to do soul-saving.

The Church today, as an instrument to bring in the body, must evangelize or perish. Without evangelization, it becomes an institution of culture and refinement, but it has NO LIFE! The more a church lives unto itself, the quicker it dies. The Church today is so busy with social activities that it has no time for its primary excuse for existence. When the fire goes out in the human body, it dies; even so with the Church. When its fires of evangelization go out, it dies. When ministers and deacons create an evangelistic atmosphere in the church, church-members will soon begin to be interested in the eternal welfare of their loved ones, friends and neighbors. Some ministers have resisted the temptation to use the pulpit for the discussion of current topics of the day. I believe not so many preachers would be in prison over in Europe if they had retained the gospel message in their pulpits instead of discussing politics.

I say some preachers believe and know they are called to preach the gospel and to win souls, and they have their reward. They have preserved an evangelical atmosphere, witnessed the conversion of sinners, maintained their congregations, and thousands of regenerated souls have come into the Church. Some say the unconverted will not come to church. If we were dead in earnest, do you think they would be outside? They would come out of curiosity to see what we had that they did not have if we were living as the gospel shows us how to live. A revival will come when God's people really want it.

Minister, are you sure that all your members are born-again, regenerated Christians? Some ask what is to become of the Church. There is a great day ahead for the Christian Church when it recovers its passion for lost souls. Men and women are restless, dissatisfied, eternally tired of pleaure—without purpose in life; they long to know the secret of life, of soul-health and happiness. They are heart-hungry. They want to know freedom, joy and peace.

If the gospel is preached in the Church, it will draw back these heart-hungry people, for the gospel is still "the power of God unto salvation to everyone that believeth."

Most people asking this question think of the material church—the organized denominations. Some suggest a new program, a broad and liberal policy; so they preach a social gospel. There is no problem at all connected with this question. By "church" is meant that living organism called in Scripture "the body of Christ," in which are all the born again, indwelt by the Holy Spirit, possessing the life of the Lord Jesus Christ. This Church's foundation is Christ, the Son of God, the Head of the body. This Church can never be defeated. "Upon this rock I will build my church; and the gates of hell shall not prevail against it" (Matt. 16:18).

This Church is not a permanent institution on this earth. She will not govern the world nor legislate for the world; she is not called upon to reform the world, nor to make the world better, nor to give the world a new program. She is not of the world even as her Head is not of this world. She is the representative of her absent Lord on earth. Her great business is to preach the gospel and through her testimony in the Spirit's power to complete the body, so that His body may be built up and edified (Eph. 4:11-13).

What will become of this true Church? When this true Church is complete, when all the elect are in, then her glorious destiny will be consummated. She will be united to Him—the Lord Jesus Christ (Eph. 1:23). He will present that Church to Himself, "a glorious church, not having spot, or wrinkle, or any such thing; but that it should be holy and without blemish" (Eph. 5:27).

"Then we which are alive and remain shall be caught up together with them in the clouds, to meet the Lord in the air: and so shall we ever be with the Lord. Wherefore comfort one another with these words" (I Thess. 4:17-18). Then this glorified Church will be forever with the Lord. She will rule and reign with Him over the earth. "He will see of the travail of his soul and be satisfied." Her members will be like Him in glory, as each individual member will be transformed into the same image. Such is the future of the Church.

The Church of the firstborn will shine as the stars at the last and be presented with joy before the Father's throne in the days of Christ's appearing.

Christendom, which has sadly departed from Christ and which is Laodicean in character and spirit, worldly in every sense of the word, also has a future. It will keep on federating till it federates itself into the final Babylon. The Lord said He would spue this church out of His mouth (Rev. 3:16).

When the Lord returns, this church (Babylonian) will be destroyed. It will be unknown in the future. The true Church will reign with Him over the earth. Then will the earth have peace.

I have tried with the help of the Lord and the guidance of the Holy Spirit to give you a Scriptural exposition of the true Church. Roman Catholicism declares itself to be the true Church in practice. From the reading of the past several pages we see from the Word of God that it is far from being the true Church. I am not an enemy, but a friend, of the Roman Catholic people; I love them and want—with God's help—to open their eyes. Let us sit in the pews of the Roman Catholic Church and examine its teachings and practice. The following evidence again will blast the assertion of this church to being the true Church. Sit with me just a few moments in the pews where I sat for at least twelve years, and let us look and see.

I have beside me a Roman Catholic Bible, which has been approved by His Eminence Cardinal Patrick Hayes, Archbishop of New York. I want to show you things in this version of the Bible that are not believed and not practiced by the Romish Church.

Remember, the true Church is founded upon the Word of God, and not the word of man.

I have said and will say again that if the Roman Catholic Church would let her people read the Bible, in six months a greater reformation would take place than that under Martin Luther. If the Roman Church would give the Bible to her people to read and teach, then we could believe she means well. The true fact remains that the Roman Church does not want her people to have the Word of God, and proves that she wants to keep her people in darkness and ignorance. If the Roman Church wanted her people to be instructed in the teachings of the Word of God, she would give them the Bible to read. "The entrance of thy words giveth light; it giveth understanding unto the simple" (Ps. 119:130).

The Roman Church knows that all fear would vanish if its followers were to read the Bible; it is fear that keeps the followers of Romish principles in subjection. When I was converted, I was afraid of what my priest would say and think. I was haunted by fear, fear, fear—that comes from bondage to sin.

Chapter II

IDOL WORSHIP

Now, let us take another of her teachings and show you a church organization which declares itself to be the true Church that Scripture speaks about and yet is far from Scripture in its teachings and practices!

The Roman Catholic Bible very clearly teaches us not to make idols and images and yet the Catholic Church makes them and heeds not her Bible or her God. My mother had an image of some saint on her dresser in a glass globe, before which we children knelt and prayed. Many Sundays before Mass I would kneel before an image and pray for my dead loved ones, then light candles that would burn throughout the Mass. My little sister escaped all this, for she never attended a Roman Catholic Church.

Let us examine, in the Roman Catholic Bible, a few verses on idols and images. Turn to Lev. 26:1 and read: "Ye shall not make to yourselves any idol or graven thing [image]."

Here it says, "Ye shall not make idols or images," yet we see how the leaders in the Roman Church pay no attention to the Word of God. In Exod. 20:4 we read, "Thou shalt not make to thy self a graven image nor the likeness of anything that is in heaven above or in the earth beneath, nor of those things that are in the waters under the earth."

The Roman Church makes idols and images of saints in heaven, the Virgin Mary, St. Joseph, Jesus, John the Baptist, St. Peter, etc. Here again the Roman Church ignores God's Word.

We feel sorry for the heathen in Africa and the Orient who worship idols, while in America 18,000,000 Roman

Catholics are doing the same thing! Some say they do not worship the image. The majority of Catholics do; I—who was in the Catholic Church for sixteen years— worshipped the image—and even kissed its feet.

We have the Bible and education and yet are being deceived by people who make light of God's Word. Isaiah says, "Their land also is full of idols; they worship the works of their hands, that which their own fingers have made: and the mean man boweth down, and the great man humbleth himself: therefore forgive them not" (Isa. 2:8-9). In I Cor. 8:4 we read that an idol is nothing in the world and that there is none other God but one.

Acts 15:20 says, "The people should abstain from pollutions of idols." In II Cor. 6:16 we read: "And what agreement hath the temple of God with idols?" I John 5:21 reads: "Little children, keep yourselves from idols." All these verses are taken from a Roman Catholic Bible; so we see why the Bible is kept from its members. Idol worship is pagan worship. God deliver us from it all. Surely that is not the practice of the children of light, the true believers who are members of the true Church, which puts Christ at the head and worships Him as the Saviour whose blood was shed for our sins. The power of the gospel delivers one from bowing down to any other god or idol.

CHAPTER III

PURGATORY

LET us proceed further with other practices of Catholicism that are not Scriptural. Purgatory is a primary principle of Catholicism, but never once in God's Word do we read of purgatory. Anthony Zeoli, a converted Roman Catholic, says that he was speaking to a Roman Catholic one day and he tried to tell him that in I Cor. 3:15 we have a picture of purgatory. Zeoli said, "How foolish." The fourteenth verse speaks of a reward. The Apostle was addressing Christians. He was not speaking of salvation by works, but of our works being tried after we are saved. We see in this passage that it speaks of our works tried after we are saved, and not of salvation. After death is the judgment (Heb. 9:27), not purgatory.

I Cor. 3:14-15: "If any man's work abide which he hath built thereupon, he shall receive a reward. If any man's work shall be burned, he shall suffer loss: but he himself shall be saved; yet so as by fire." Heb. 9:27: "And as it is appointed unto men once to die, but after this the judgment." Purgatory is a downright, barefaced falsehood, an invention of man inspired by Satan for the destruction of souls. The Roman Church makes slaves of her people on earth and after death makes merchandise of their souls. Yes, even "the merchandise of gold, and silver . . . and slaves, and souls of men" (Rev. 18:12-13). Prayers or money after death cannot save you, for the Word of God shows it. Two of my relatives died within six months of one another. Mother was told that they were in purgatory for seven years and the way to get them out so that they could have access to heaven was to light two candles before Mass each Sunday and have

them burn through Mass; drop fifty cents in the slot; do
this faithfully for the seven years, and they would be
allowed entrance to heaven.

Is this Scriptural? No; a thousand times NO! The
word *purgatory* is not found in the Bible. It not only is
not found in the King James Version but is not in the
Douay Version which the Roman Catholics use. The
doctrine of purgatory was not known in the first century;
so we see it is not a doctrine of Christianity. Not a verse,
word, or phrase is to be found in either version of the
Bible in support of the doctrine of purgatory. A priest
told me that this doctrine is in the apocryphal and non-
canonical Book of the Maccabees, *but* the fact is that although the Jews today have prayers for the dead, they
do not believe that their dead are in purgatory, and, also,
in these prayers they exalt the God of heaven in the
sorrow of their bereavement.

In the early Christian Church there was no purgatory.
Christians were persecuted then by pagan Rome, and
thousands of Christians went to the stake with faith in
their hearts that they would go to Jesus in heaven. There
was no such doctrine in the Catholic Church for six
hundred years. Pope Gregory the Great, in the year
600 A.D., was the first to form the concept of purgatory
as a third state in which souls could be purified before
entrance into heaven—an idea derived from Plato and
Virgil. So we see it has a pagan origin. But even then
it did not become a dogma of the Church of Rome until
in 1459 it was accepted by the Council of Florence, and
confirmed by the Council of Trent in 1548.

Christians accept the Word of God—not the theories of
man—as a foundation. This doctrine further teaches
that the soul in purgatory can do nothing toward its own
deliverance and is dependent upon prayers and Masses
said by the living. Larkin, in *Rightly Dividing the Word*,
says that the purpose of the doctrine was to secure

revenue for the church by so working on the sympathy of loved ones that they would pay for "Masses" to deliver the souls of their relatives and friends from the torments of purgatory.

The doctrine of purgatory nullifies the efficacy of Christ's sacrifice on the cross. We are jealous of the honor due to Christ. "The blood of Jesus Christ cleanseth us from all sin" (I John 1:7). Rome says Christ forgives the guilt of sin but not the penalty thereof, which must be atoned for in the flames of purgatory. The doctrine makes the priest more powerful than God Himself, for he has the key to purgatory and has power to liberate that soul at any time and smuggle it into heaven. This is cruel, as the priest will not say the prayer and will not read the mass unless he is paid for it, which makes him seem to be a cruel and heartless person. It makes God appear to be a heartless judge, for He still sends forgiven souls of people to purgatory to burn for small sins—after giving His Son as an atonement on the cross. How can you reconcile that doctrine with a God of love? After a good Catholic has received absolution, holy communion, the extreme unction, the holy water over his dead body at the Requiem Mass in the church, and is buried in consecrated ground—all this does not free him from the flames of purgatory.

Why do Catholics dread the hour of death? Because the good Catholic has before him the fire of purgatory, and the bad one has the fire of hell. A dying Roman Catholic has no assurance that his sins are forgiven and that he is going to Jesus, who paid the penalty for them in His death on the cross. When I die, as I am not a Roman Catholic, I will not go to purgatory and I will not go to hell, for I am not traveling that way. This doctrine is cruel to the loved ones left behind. They have no consolation in picturing their loved ones in the flames of purgatory. Thank God, there is no such prison!

Then they say that the suffrages of the living can help the souls in purgatory by alleviating their pains. These suffrages are in the form of credits or indulgences, and can be earned by good works performed and prayers recited in this life, either by the Catholic himself while living, or by his family and friends after death, or by having priests read masses for him; these credits will be applied to shorten his pains. The Council decrees that "whosoever doubts this doctrine, and says that Christ justifies the sinner and cleanses him from all sin, without leaving the penalty to be expiated either in this world or purgatory, let him be accursed."

Then St. John and St. Paul would both be accursed for listening to them: "The blood of Jesus Christ . . . cleanseth us from *all sin*" (I John 1:7), and St. Paul says "There is therefore now no condemnation to them which are in Christ Jesus" (Rom. 8:1).

I shall quote from a tract which is one in a group called "Why I am a Catholic Series"; the title of this particular tract is "Purgatory Saves Even the Best Christians from Hell."

Purgatory, so says this tract by the Catholic writer, "is the middle state between heaven and hell, where souls who have died in venial sin, or who have not yet done penance for their forgiven sins, must for a time undergo purification by suffering. To some the very name 'purgatory' awakens old prejudices which centuries have instilled into them." It goes on to say, "But, there must be such a spiritual hospital."

The reader who is a careful student of the Word of God will fully realize that the preceding quotation from the tract is nothing more than foolish speculation. Nowhere in the Bible do we have one reference to what the Catholics call a "spiritual hospital." Nowhere in the New Testament do we read that one must undergo temporary purification by suffering because he died in venial sin.

A man who dies without the Lord Jesus Christ as His Saviour, is lost forever. Physical death ends all opportunities to become saved. The Bible clearly states, "Now is the accepted time; now is the day of salvation." NOT in the hereafter, as the Church of Rome would have us believe. Christ spoke about a hell for the unsaved and a heaven for those who were and would trust in HIM. Nowhere in Scripture do we read about a middle state. The Lord Jesus Christ never spoke about a middle state as the Catholic Church calls it.

The Scriptures plainly teach, as we read in I Cor. 15:3, "Christ died for OUR sins according to the scriptures." Romans 5:6 says, "When we were yet without strength, in due time Christ died for the ungodly." Christ died for our past, present and future sins. One must remember that when He died on the cross more than nineteen hundred years ago, He died for you. All your sins were yet future, but Christ died for them. The moment I accept HIM as my personal Saviour, I am saved from not only *some* sins but *all* sins; they are put under HIS blood, never again to be remembered. Of course, when we sin in our present living, our hearts should be turned to God in confession, for the Scripture says that "if we confess our sins, HE is faithful and just to forgive us our sins, and to cleanse us from all unrighteousness" (I John 1:9). If a Christian dies suddenly with some unconfessed sin in his life, he is still saved, and not lost because of that sin, whatever it may be; for when he became a Christian, Christ saved him from past sins, present sins and future sins. Those transgressions are already forgiven under His blood; those sins have already been judged and forgiven through Christ's finished work on the cross.

The sin question was settled once and for all. After a person becomes a Christian, he will never be judged for sin or sins; Christ once and for all paid the penalty of our sins—which was death. At the judgment seat of

Christ, Christians will be judged for their works, for their deeds done in the body—not for their sins. If one is to be judged for his sins in eternity, as the Catholic believes that there must be temporary suffering for sins, then the Lord Jesus Christ to him is an insufficient Saviour. Christ then, according to the teachings of the Church of Rome, died for *some* sins, and NOT FOR ALL, since Catholics preach suffering for some sins after death. But according to the word of God I read, in Ephesians 1:7, "In whom we have redemption through HIS BLOOD, even the forgiveness of sins." John 1:12: "But as many as received HIM, to them gave he power to become the sons of God, even to them that believe on HIS name." Shall sons of God suffer for sin, then? Ah, no, my reader, not according to the precious Word of God. Read and study carefully the preceding verses. Another verse that will reveal the fallacy of purgatory (temporary suffering for sins) is found in John 5:24: "Verily, verily, I say unto you, he that heareth my word and believeth on him that sent me, HATH EVERLASTING LIFE, and shall not come INTO CONDEMNATION; but is passed from death unto life." You see, my friend, there is no suffering for sins; there is no condemnation; for through Christ, condemnation was lifted from the sinner once and for all when he became a Christian by accepting the Lord Jesus as his personal Saviour. Christ suffered *once* for sins (I Pet. 3:18); for the Christian there is no more suffering for sins. Christ did that.

Here is a further quotation from the "Why I Am a Catholic Series"; it is an excerpt from "Purgatory in the New Testament": "After warning his hearers to beware lest they be suddenly delivered to the Judge and cast into prison, the Saviour adds: 'I say to thee, thou shalt not come out thence, till thou hast paid the last farthing' (Matt. 5:25-26). Here Christ speaks of a prison in the other world, in which souls are detained until divine justice has been fully satisfied."

Now, let us quote the preceding Scripture in full, exactly as we find it in God's Word. "Agree with thine adversary quickly, while thou art in the way with him; lest at any time the adversary deliver thee to the judge, and the judge deliver thee to the officer, and thou be cast into prison. Verily, I say unto thee, Thou shalt by no means come out thence, till thou hast paid the uttermost farthing." Here Christ is speaking against carrying petty differences into court. The Jews are still living under the law, and from verse 17 to the end of this quoted chapter, Christ is xpounding His relationship to the law. In these particular verses, He is explaining how to get along with one's enemies. The adversary spoken of here is a common antagonist, and Christ is saying: "Come to an agreement with him lest he swear out a warrant and have you arrested and brought before a judge, for if the judge's decision is not in your favor, you will be delivered to prison by an officer." ("Prison" refers to an ordinary prison here on the earth—not in the other world.) "You then must serve your term in prison." This is precisely the system of punishment which we have today.

I quote again from this same tract from the discussion entitled "Purgatory in the New Testament": "Notice the lack of assurance in the following words "There seems to be a reference to purgatory also in the words of St. Paul in I Cor. 3:11-15: 'For other foundation can no man lay than that is laid, which is Jesus Christ. Now if any man build upon this foundation gold, silver, precious stones, wood, hay, stubble; every man's work shall be made manifest: for the day shall declare it, because it shall be revealed by fire; and the fire shall try every man's work of what sort it is. If any man's work abide which he hath built thereupon, he shall receive a reward. If any man's work shall be burned, he shall suffer loss; but he himself shall be saved; yet so as by fire.' These words indicate a process of purgation by which a man's deeds are tested.

There is no test needed in heaven; no one can be saved in hell. Hence the fire that fits a man's soul for heaven must be similar to what Catholics for that very reason call 'Purgatory'."

The above may seem very convincing, but let us notice the following things. The writer of this tract says, "There seems to be a reference to purgatory in the words of St. Paul in I Cor. 3:11-15"—a very definite indication that they are not sure about it; in other words, they are speculating and using the Scripture to try to prove a doctrine which cannot be found in the Word of God.

Let us consider again the portion of Scripture used: I Cor. 3:11-15. "For other foundation can no man lay than that is laid, which is Jesus Christ. Now if any man build upon this foundation gold, silver, precious stones, wood, hay, stubble; every man's work shall be made manifest: for the day shall declare it, because it shall be revealed by fire; and the fire shall try every man's work of what sort it is. If any man's work abide which he hath built there-upon, he shall receive a reward. If any man's work shall be burned, he shall suffer loss, but he himself shall be saved; yet so as by fire." Here Paul is speaking about the only foundation for salvation, which is the Lord Jesus Christ (verse 11): "Other foundation can no man lay than that is laid, which is Jesus Christ." In Ephesians 2:8-9 we find the same message differently worded: "For by grace are ye saved through faith (in Christ); and that not of yourselves: it is the gift of God: *not of works*, lest any man should boast." We are not saved by works, but through faith to believe in Christ and accept Him as our Saviour. After we are saved, it is our duty to work for God and to serve Him.

Verses 12, 13, 14 and 15, have to do with man's works after he has become a Christian, and does not refer to salvation, as the foregoing quotation from the tract would lead one to believe. Verse 14 says: "If any man's work abide which he hath built thereupon, he shall receive a *reward*." God, in the New Testament Scriptures, offers to the lost, the unsaved, salvation as a *free gift,* and for the faithful service of the saved man or woman, a reward. We cannot buy God's eternal salvation through works, for it is not for sale. Salvation is a free gift, while rewards are earned by works; Matthew 10:42: "And whosoever shall give to drink unto one of these little ones a cup of cold water only in the name of a disciple, verily I say unto you, he shall in no wise lose his reward." Also notice II Timothy 4:7-8: "I have fought a good fight, I have finished my course, I have kept the faith: Henceforth there is laid up for me a crown of righteousness, which the Lord, the righteous judge, shall give me at that day: and not to me only, but unto all them also that love his appearing." Observe Luke 19:17 and I Cor. 9:24 also.

The word "purgatory" can neither be found in, nor proven from, the Scripture. The Word of God speaks of a heaven for those who are His and a place called hell for every unbeliever.

I will now quote from a booklet called "What the Catholic Church Is and What She Teaches"; from page 33, under the heading, "Purgatory and Prayer for the Dead," I quote: "We know nothing with certainty about purgatory, except the fact of its existence, and that it involves a delay in entering heaven till the last relics of sinfulness are purged away. We are told nothing of the amount, kind, or duration of its purgative process." This quotation involves a confession of the lack of knowledge concerning purgatory, and manifests marked uncertainty. Yet much of the teaching of Catholicism is based on this uncertain doctrine; the practice of praying for the dead is particularly dependent upon this doctrine. Catholics must make the confession that they know nothing certain concerning "purgatory," because there is not one verse of

Scripture to support the assertions and teachings concerning it.

The Catholic Church maintains she does not encourage her followers to read the Bible so that it will not be abused. Certainly these uncertain teachings come close to abusing the Word of God! There can be no middle ground called "purgatory," for no reference to it can be found in the Bible. And no man or group has the right to add to the Word of God, or to take away from it.

Let us quote some Scripture:

"Then shall the dust return to the earth as it was: and the spirit shall return unto God who gave it" (Eccles. 12:7).

"Though I walk through the valley of the shadow of death, I will fear no evil: for thou art with me ... Surely goodness and mercy shall follow me all the days of my life: and I will dwell in the house of the Lord for ever" (Ps. 23).

Jesus said nothing about purgatory. He talked about heaven and hell. He says in John 14:1-4: "Let not your hearts be troubled, you believe in God, believe also in me. In my Father's house there are many mansions: if it were not so I would have told you. I go and prepare a place for you. And if I go and prepare a place for you, I will come again and will take you to myself; that where I am, you also may be" (Douay Version).

In Luke 23:43 Jesus speaks to the thief on the cross when he repented: "Verily I say unto thee, Today shalt thou be with me in paradise."

St. Stephen, the first Christian martyr, just before his death saw the heavens open and the Son of Man standing on the right hand of God. "And they stoned Stephen, invoking and saying: Lord Jesus, receive my spirit."

Paul says, "I have fought a good fight, I have finished my course, I have kept the faith. As to the rest, there is laid up for me a crown of justice which the Lord the righteous judge will render to me in that day." There is no mention of purgatory, for Paul expected to be with the Lord at death. St. Peter had the same faith. "Blessed be the God, and Father of our Lord Jesus Christ which according to his abundant mercy hath begotten us again unto a lively hope by the resurrection of Jesus Christ from the dead; to an inheritance incorruptible and undefiled . . . reserved in heaven for you" (I Pet. 1:3-4).

The doctrine of purgatory is unscriptural. There is no intermediate place—only heaven and hell; the impassable gulf is fixed, and the Bible declares that there is no possibility of the occupants of hell ever passing over into heaven. This nullifies the doctrine of purgatory as preached by the Romish Church. How can a religious (so called) system with such unscriptural practices ever declare itself to be the true Church? The doctrine of purgatory had its origin in the belief that the souls of men when they die are not fit to go immediately to heaven; so an "intermediate place" was invented where they might wait for awhile and be purged of their sins. The instrument of purification was physical suffering.

Oh, the fallacy of this; Were not Jesus' sufferings on the cross enough? Don't men believe in His finished work? What the Christian world needs, the greatest need of the hour, is less of man's guesses and more of God's messages.

"Because there is wrath, beware lest he take thee away with his stroke [death]: then a great ransom cannot deliver thee. Will he esteem thy riches? no, not gold, nor all the forces of strength" (Job 36:18-19). "None of them can by any means redeem his brother, nor give to God a ransom for him," the Word says (Ps. 49:7-8). "None of them can by any means redeem his brother, nor give to God a ransom for him: for the redemption of their soul is precious, and it ceaseth for ever."

"Forasmuch as ye know that ye were not redeemed with corruptible things, as silver and gold, from your vain conversation received by tradition from your fathers; but with the precious blood of Christ" (I Pet. 1:18-19).

Surely paying money for the dead is not in the Bible and is not practiced by believing Christians who are true to its teachings. This is an imposition that should be earnestly condemned. The priest who tells a sorrowing father and mother that their children are suffering in a place called purgatory and that his prayers, paid for with cash in hand, are necessary for the release of their souls from this man-made purgatory, is imposing upon them, and is false to the teachings of Christ. It is almost unbelievable to know that this deception is being practiced among sane, civilized people.

O God, open the eyes of the blind; show them as you did me how far from Scripture, Catholicism has drifted!

If a Roman Catholic dies and has no money left for Masses to be said for his soul, he may suffer in purgatory and be cast into hell so far as the priests are concerned. The priest, in order to get money from these deceived people, has two Masses—High and Low—for souls in purgatory. The High Mass costs from ten to one hundred dollars or more, according to the display of flowers and candles and the number of priests taking part. The Low Mass costs about five dollars; only six candles are used, and it is sung in a low voice. The High Mass is sung in a loud tone of voice. Of course, even if one be poor he will save enough money for a High Mass, thinking it will be more effective. One is as good as the other; and they are both good for nothing.

It is high money—High Mass; it is low money—Low Mass; it is no money—no Mass. The following is taken from a tract by Theodore E. Beebe:

Money for masses, but who ever read
Where we're told in the Bible to pray for the dead?
Or the soul after death is cleansed from its stain,
Or through masses relieved from suffering and pain?

Money for masses, now we see well,
To die saved is heaven, if lost, it is hell.
It is here the blood cleanses, not after we die,
It is here Jesus saves, and prepares for the sky.

Money for masses; oh! what a sham,
A trick of the devil, the millions to damn,
Here only the soul from all sin is made free,
For no one can read GOD'S WORD and not see.

Money for masses, but time will expire,
And the last priest will die, and enter the fire.
And we want to know, if you can explain,
How he'll be prayed out when no priest remains.

Money for masses, hang on to your purse.
Let the priest threaten, condemn, and then curse;
Take GOD'S WORD as your guide, it is safest and best,
Trust in Jesus, then, dying, you'll enter His rest.

Oh, that the day may soon come when God will put an end to all this. "Ye are not redeemed by corruptible things, as silver and gold, but with the precious blood of Christ" (I Pet. 1:18-19; also see Jer. 23:11 and Zeph. 3:4).

For the few moments that you have been sitting in the pews of Catholicism, many of you are surprised at its teachings. Remember, with God's help, I want to lead you into the truth, not away from it; John 8:32: "Ye shall know the truth, and the truth shall make you free."

Many of you are disquieted because of the few moments during which you have been sitting with me in the pews of popish and Romish power and authority. Sit with me for a few more minutes, Christian friend, unsaved one and Roman Catholic, as we deal with confession, the Virgin Mary worship, Peter's marriage, bishops and priests.

In this study I am trying to show you the true Church and to reveal the doctrines and practices of the Church of Rome, which are far from being Scriptural. Its teachings are so contradictory to the Bible's teaching, so far removed from Holy Writ, that it is absurd to claim that the Roman Church is the true Church.

The true Church is founded upon the Word of God; its commission is to preach the Word, to uphold Jesus as the Saviour from sin, for He is the Head of the true Church, which is composed of "born-again" believers.

CHAPTER IV

CONFESSION OF SINS TO . . . ?

LET us with Christian love and sympathy for blinded people consider the teaching of confession of sins to the priest. This practice of confessing sins to the priest, is also contradictory to the teachings of the Roman Catholic Bible. The teachings of Catholicism are built upon the word of man, rather than the Word of God. Let us look for a few more minutes at the teaching of confession of sins to the priest.

In the Roman Catholic Church the people confess their sins to the priest, kneel down before him in the confessional and there tell him the secret sins of their lives. Here is where the Romish Church holds a powerful sway over the individual. For six years, every other week, I ignorant of the Word of God which teaches that Jesus became our sin-bearer, confessed my sins to a priest. Even in the Roman Catholic Bible, confession is not taught, which again we see is far removed from Scripture. In Esdras 10:10-11 we read (Douay Version): "And Esdras, the priest, stood up and said to them: 'Ye have transgressed and taken strange wives to add to the sins of Israel and now make confession to the Lord God of your Fathers.'" It does not say here that the priest told them, the people, to confess to *him;* he told them to confess to *God.* In Acts 8:22 Peter says to Simon, "Repent, therefore, of this thy wickedness, and pray God if perhaps the thought of thine heart may be forgiven thee." Here in this verse Peter says, "Pray to God," not "Confess to me or a priest."

In Acts 10:25-26 we read: "As Peter was coming in, Cornelius met him, and fell down at his feet and worshipped him. But Peter took him up, saying, Stand up; I myself also am a man!" Here we see that Peter would not let anyone bow down to him or confess to him. His words were, "Stand up; I myself also am a man"—not pope nor priest, but a man.

On the day of Pentecost, Peter told the people to believe the gospel and be saved and not to confess to him. In Heb. 10:11 we read, "And every priest standeth daily ministering and offering oftentimes the same sacrifices, which can never take away sins." In this verse we see that a priest can neither forgive sins nor make sacrifices. In Heb. 10:10 we read that Jesus is the sacrifice once and for all; therefore there remains no other. Read also I John 1:9. It is a known fact that the priest through the power of the confessional knows more about many of his followers than husbands know of their own wives.

How can the Roman Church claim to be the true Church with such a practice?

A young Roman Catholic girl was in my meetings, and she told me that she must confess it to the priest for it was a sin. Such a practice is not in Scripture. The true church (God's redeemed ones) loves His Word and applies the teachings of the Scripture to the individual life.

The thought that the Roman Church is the only Church —and, yes, the true Church—is a far-fetched one. The followers of this religion, who believe this, lack a knowledge of the Word of God and the meaning of the death of Christ. Scripture teaches that He became our sin-bearer. He is our mediator between God and man because He paid the penalty for our sins, which is death. Scripture teaches that He is the last and only sacrifice to remove sin. He died for my sin; therefore my confession is to Him (I John 2:2; Acts 10:4; John 3:18, 5:24).

Nowhere in Scripture are we told that the priest has power to remove and forgive sins. We again see the works of man, the guesses of man, and not the message of God's Word in this practice. The priest declares himself to be the mediator between God and man. Yet the Bible teaches that "there is one mediator between God and men, the man Christ Jesus" (I Tim. 2:5).

Chapter V

TRANSUBSTANTIATION, OR THE LORD'S SUPPER

Let us now consider their teaching in regard to the Lord's Supper: "For as often as ye eat this bread, and drink this cup, ye do shew the Lord's death till he come" (I Cor. 11:26). We know the Lord's Supper is not a permanent ordinance. It will be discontinued when the Lord returns. It is a memorial. First it looks back to the cross, and then forward to His coming. When Christ instituted the Communion, or the Lord's Supper, He gave bread and wine to His disciples (I Cor. 11:24-25). The Roman Catholic Church does not give bread (the symbol of His broken body) nor wine (the symbol of His shed blood) to her people, as the Scripture teaches.

The Mass is the most important ceremony of the Roman Catholic Church. And it is the largest income-producing ceremony also. The Mass is purported to be a representation of the Lord's Supper. But what a difference between the Mass as it is said today in the Roman Church and the Lord's Supper as instituted by our Lord and practiced by the Early Church! There is nothing evil in the mass itself; on the contrary, it is beautiful in its prayers, Bible verses, portions of Scripture, excerpts from the Epistles; if it were in English, it would edify and instruct. The prayers are all addressed to God and end with the name of the Lord Jesus Christ. None are addressed to saints or to Mary. Not the Mass itself but the doctrine concerning it is objectionable. Let us look at a few of the differences between the Mass and the Lord's Supper. The text of I Cor. 11:23-26 in the Douay Version is virtually the same as the King James. The Lord's Supper was celebrated in the evening. In the Roman Church the

Mass must be celebrated only in the morning; only by special dispensation can a priest say Mass after twelve o'clock noon, and never after one o'clock.

It was instituted after supper. In the Roman Church the priest and the people must fast from midnight to the moment of Communion. We do not say the stomach must be void of food, but that the soul be void of sin before we partake.

The Lord's Supper contained both bread and wine. In the Mass no bread is used, but a wafer that must not be chewed and must be swallowed whole, or allowed to melt in the mouth. We partake of the bread from the loaf and eat it and are nourished by it.

In Matt. 26:27-28 the Word says, "Taking the chalice, he gave thanks; and gave to them, saying, Drink ye all of this. For this is my blood of the New Testament which shall be shed for many unto remission of sins." In the Mass there is the chalice, but only the priest has it. It was the Council of Constance (1414 A. D.) that took the chalice from the people, for during the previous fourteen hundred years the Catholic Church gave the chalice to the people.

The Lord's Supper was a Communion of Christ with all the disciples. In the Mass only the priest communes. Christ was seated at the same table with His disciples and was talking with them. In the Mass the priest sets himself apart from the people and has his back to them. The minister should come down and sit at the Communion table with the people.

The doctrine of transubstantiation—one of the paramount doctrines of the Catholic Church—seems to be very mysterious. Let us examine it in the light of the Word of God.

I quote again from a Catholic authority, citing material from pages 14, 22, and 24 of the book called, "What the

Catholic Church Teaches." This has to do with what the Catholic Church believes and teaches in regard to the "Eucharist" (the Lord's Supper), also called Transubstantiation, or the Sacrifice of the Mass.

I quote the following: "The Eucharist, or Lord's Supper, as it is called by the Protestants, is the sacrament for supplying our souls with the nourishment of spiritual food. It is believed that when the formulas of consecration are pronounced, the words of Christ, 'this is my body,' 'this is my blood,' are literally fulfilled, so that what were previously bread and wine became really and truly Christ's body and blood. There is no deception of the senses, for all the properties of bread and wine that can be discovered by inspection remain as before; and yet the things themselves are no longer bread and wine, but Christ's body and blood concealed under those appearances. It is an invisible miracle and a mystery; but still greater is the mystery of divine condescension, which thus brings Christ down among us, and into a most real, intimate and mystical union with our souls.

"It follows that since Christ is really present in the sacred elements, He can and ought to be adored there; just as He would be adored if He came again on earth in His natural human form. Hence the church causes the sacred Host (as the consecrated bread is termed) to be reserved in the tabernacles of the churches, not only for the use of the sick, but to enable the faithful to pay their devotion to Christ there present. The service of benediction is an act of this kind of reverence, the sacred Host being then exhibited on the altar for adoration. Processions of the blessed sacrament are another form of this devotion."

The preceding discussion is very wordy. It is the teaching of the Catholic Church regarding the doctrine of the Lord's Supper. I desire in the following paragraph to show you how contrary it is to the teachings of this doctrine in the Word of God. On page 24 of "The Catholic Authority" we read, "The idea [the sacrifice of the Mass] is sublime, but difficult to explain." Such a confession on the part of the writer ought to make us search and think. In all that I have quoted there is not one verse of Scripture to prove what has been asserted. Let us now turn to the precious Word of God, the Bible, "For as often as ye eat this bread, and drink this cup, ye do shew the Lord's death till he come" (I Cor. 11:26).

The Lord's Supper is a proclamation of a past act, the pronouncement of a present experience, the prophecy of a future event.

Those who sit at the Lord's Table are to turn their opened eyes of faith back to the cross, are to lift up their opened eyes to Christ's coming again and are to open their hearts of love to fellowship with His Spirit.

The Lord's Supper deals with believers in three tenses: past, present and future.

As to the past, it is a *commemoration*.

As to the present, it is a *meditation*.

As to the future, it is an *anticipation*.

At the present moment we are concerned with the Lord's Supper only as it relates to the past, as a commemoration of that scene enacted upon the cross of Calvary.

It is the privilege and duty of every child of God to join in the proclamation of that glorious gospel of God's grace, namely, the good news of Christ's death for the redemption of man.

Jesus commanded this as the sublime privilege and supreme obligation of every believer.

"Go ye, therefore, and teach all nations, baptizing them in the name of the Father, and of the Son, and of the Holy Ghost."

The inspired Paul commends the proclamation of the gospel as the highest honor and distinction of a Christian church.

There are many methods of proclaiming this good news of how Christ died for our sins according to the Scriptures.

It may be done by personal testimony. "Ye shall be witnesses unto me." Every Christian, every day of his life, should bear joyous testimony to what Christ has done for him in the salvation of his soul.

This gospel may be proclaimed by public preaching. Happy indeed should that man be who has been so honored and exalted of God as to be called divinely and set apart as a chosen vessel to proclaim His message among the people!

This gospel may be proclaimed by singing its message. Multitudes can bear testimony to the fact that the message of life and light and love has been borne to their hearts by some gospel song.

The gospel may be proclaimed by the distribution of religious literature. Many are the stories and marvelous are the results which have come to the kingdom of God in the conversion of souls by some wisely placed piece of Christian truth.

The gospel may be proclaimed by the giving of money for the sending of missionaries.

The gospel may be proclaimed by the living of a holy life.

The gospel may be proclaimed over the telegraph, on the telephone and by radio. All modern inventions were intended by God to be conveyors of His message to mankind.

But not all are called to be preachers, nor can all be singers, nor can all give large sums of money, nor is the radio available to all.

There must be one way then by which each and every disciple may proclaim the message of the gospel, and that is through the Lord's Table.

The Lord's Supper is a commemoration of the death of Christ. "Do this in remembrance of me," or "in commemoration of me" (Douay). In the Roman Church, however, the Mass is not a commemoration, but it is a sacrifice, a renewal of the actual crucifixion of our Lord. The Roman Church promulgated the doctrine of transubstantiation in 1212, and the Council of Trent in 1536 A.D. made it final, which means that when the priest pronounces the five words of consecration, *"Hoc est enim corpus meum,"* over the wafer, the wafer is immediately changed into the actual body, blood, soul, divinity, of our Lord. And whoever denies or doubts this doctrine "let him be accursed" (Sess. 13).

You must have faith that the wafer is not the symbol of but the real living body of our Lord—the same body that hung on the cross of Calvary.

How true the Word of God is in Isa. 28:7: "But they also have erred through wine, and through strong drink are out of the way; the priest and the prophet have erred through strong drink, they are swallowed up of wine, they are out of the way through strong drink; they err in vision, they stumble in judgment." Read also Jer. 23:11.

Again we see another practice of the Romish Church which is not Scriptural, according to the words from their own Bible. God, deliver us from error and man-made doctrine. "The Word [the Bible] is a lamp unto my feet and a light unto my path." Our Christian living and doctrines come from the Scripture, and not from the mouth of man. Sit with me for a little while longer while I take you into some of the other teachings, giving you a bird's eye view. I know you must be convinced already that the Roman Church is not the true Church of the Bible, for she does not even teach the things within her own Bible.

Let us consider the subject of bishops. The Roman Catholic Bible says, "A faithful saying—if a man desire the office of a bishop, he desireth good works. It behooveth therefore a bishop to be harmless, the husband of one wife; one that ruleth well his own house, having his children in subjection with all charity" (I Tim. 3:1-4). It is very plainly written here that he be the husband of one wife. Where is the rule of celibacy? Here is another reason the Bible is kept from the people—they might find out that the practices of the church do not follow their own Bible. A bishop of the Roman Catholic Church is not the husband of one wife and is not the bishop described in this passage.

The Roman Catholic Church teaches her people to call the priest "Father." How many times I did this, not knowing the fallacy of it! Yet in her Bible it says, "And call none your father upon earth for one is your Father who is in heaven" (Matt. 23:9). It says very plainly, "Call no one, or no man, Father." This means priest, pope and all in religious circles. Again we see error and unscriptural teaching. The true Church is built upon the Word of God; the Bible is her foundation. This foundation is not to be found in Catholicism, which gives us facts to prove that she is not the true Church, but a religious organization and a great money-making system to keep people in darkness. Oh, that we might pray: "Lord, open thou mine eyes, that I may behold wondrous things out of thy law" (Ps. 119:18).

CHAPTER VI

WAS PETER POPE?

JUST two questions more: Was Peter pope? And what about the Virgin Mary? Let us consult our Roman Catholic Bible and read whether or not Peter was pope. Take, for instance, I Pet. 1:1: "Peter, an *apostle* of Jesus Christ" [not pope]. In Gal. 2:9 we read that Peter was a *pillar of the church* [not pope]. Paul considers himself Peter's equal. He says, "I was not a whit behind the very chiefest apostles." Read II Cor. 11:5. If Peter had been a pope, would Paul have dared to speak after this fashion? Paul also rebuked Peter when he came to Antioch. Paul said, "I withstood him to the face, because he was to be blamed." Read Gal. 2:11-16. If Peter had been pope, how would Paul have dared to rebuke him openly for failing to practice what he preached in his action toward the Gentiles?

No writer of the New Testament speaks of Peter as pope. What does the silence mean? Can it be a conspiracy against him? Why did they ignore his authority? Why? *Because Peter was never pope.* All the Apostles were brethren. The only time Peter acted like a pope was when he used the sword and cut off the ear of Malchus (John 18:10). Popes have often made use of arms. Paul says, "But when I saw that they walked not uprightly according to the truth of the gospel, I said unto Peter before them all, If thou, being a Jew, livest after the manner of Gentiles, and not as do the Jews, why compellest thou the Gentiles to live as do the Jews? (Gal. 2:14) Popes have done the same thing for centuries. Peter also opposed the teaching of Christ in Matt. 16:21-23. In this respect all popes have excelled. This was all the popery

Peter had in him. Christ delivered him from the power of the Evil One.

Peter was sent to preach by others (Acts 8:14). This does not seem pope-like. Instead of sending others to preach, he is sent himself. Peter did not preside at the council in Jerusalem. He did not call the council or open its deliberations, but James took the direction of the gathering. If Peter were pope, why did he not show his authority? (Acts 15).

Butler's *Catholic Catechism* (pages 45-46) contains the following:

"Who is the visible head of the Church? To whom does the Pope succeed as visible head of the Church?

"To St. Peter who was the chief of the apostles, Christ's vicar on earth, the first Pope and Bishop of Rome."

The Roman Church's teaching must be wrong in this, for Peter was not sent to Rome. It was Paul who was sent by Jesus to Rome, and not Peter (read Acts 23:11). Peter preached to the Jews and preached the gospel of circumcision (Gal. 2:7-8).

In the "Catholic Observer" appeared the following: "St. Peter was married before he became an apostle, but *ceased* to live with his wife when he was elevated to the office and dignity of the Christian priesthood."

A certain paper very quickly answered this slander against Peter by saying, "If Peter ceased to live with his wife, one of them must have left the other; if it were the wife, then St. Peter must have been a poor foundation for a church. If on the other hand, St. Peter did the leaving, then he was a wife deserter; then the Roman Church was founded upon a wife deserter. We know Peter did not leave his wife." Paul makes it plain that after Peter became an apostle, he still had his wife. He says, "Have we not power to lead about a sister, a wife, as well as other apostles, and as the brethren of the Lord, and Cephas?" (I Cor. 9:5) Was Peter ever a pope?

The Roman Church for centuries has been digging for information to prove their assertions, but as yet they have found none and never will. Therefore, Benedict XV is not Peter's successor, and consequently the whole papal fabric falls to pieces.

The Roman Catholic Church declares itself to be built upon Peter. Notice very carefully that its head is a man —a sinful man who had many faults. How can Catholicism claim to be the true Church? In Scripture we are told that the true Church (all who believe) is built upon Christ (I Cor. 3:11). Read church history and you will find that between the eighth and fourteenth centuries there were rival popes, at one time three and at another time two—all declaring their right to be pope.

I thank God that all believers who have been washed in His blood and who by faith have confessed Him as their sin-bearer are founded upon a sure foundation that is Jesus Christ. When a church is built on a man, or around a man, it will fail. But Christ is the foundation and the Head of the true Church. When Catholicism preaches that its church is built upon Peter, it contradicts the teachings of Scripture and cannot be the true church.

> My hope is built on nothing less
> Than Jesus' blood and righteousness;
> I dare not trust the sweetest frame,
> But wholly lean on Jesus' name.
>
> When darkness seems to hide His face,
> I rest on His unchanging grace;
> In ev'ry high and stormy gale,
> My anchor holds within the veil.
>
> On Christ, the solid Rock, I stand;
> All other ground is sinking sand,
> All other ground is sinking sand.

CHAPTER VII

MARY WORSHIP

LET us see what the Romish Church teaches about the Virgin Mary. Many of you by the Scriptural evidence produced have seen that the declarations of Rome that she is the true Church are contrary to Scripture. Let every man be a liar, but let God's Word be true.

Sit with me, please, in the pews of Catholicism a little longer. We shall not stay here, but let us examine its teaching about the Virgin Mary. Then we shall sum up all of it in conclusion to show you the work of man's hands, the inventions carried out and the practices in Catholicism which are far removed from Scriptural teaching.

I desire in this section of the book to show you the fallacy of worshipping Mary. I will show you the book called, "What the Catholic Church Is and What She Teaches." Let us look at page 30 under the heading, "Devotion to Our Lady." The main idea being clear, we can deal more in detail with the church's doctrine concerning Our Lady. It may be summed up briefly under three heads: first, Mary is the mother of God and man. Secondly, she takes an interest in the faithful on earth. Thirdly, it is legitimate and becoming to honor her, and ask for her prayers.

To Mary there is also applied the doctrine of the "immaculate conception" which means that she was without sin, "sinless."

I would like also to quote from a book called "The Glories of Mary" which was written by Cardinal Alphonsus di Liguori, one of the greatest devotional writers of the Catholic Church. The editor's notice says:

"Everything that our saint has written is, as it were, a summary of a Catholic tradition on the subject that it treats: it is not an individual author; it is, so to speak, the church herself that speaks to us by the voice of her prophets, her apostles, her pontiffs, her saints, her fathers, her doctors of all nations and all ages. This book is approved by James Cardinal Gibbons, Archbishop of Baltimore.

I desire now to contrast for you what the Catholic Church teaches about Mary and what the Bible has to say. We believe the Word of God to be final in any matter of Christian doctrine—not the word of man, or a group of men, or a church.

THE ROMAN CATHOLIC CHURCH:

"And SHE is truly made a mediatress of peace between sinners and God."

Sinners receive pardon by . . . Mary ALONE" (pages 75, 76).

"Mary is our life."

"To understand why the holy Church makes us call Mary our life . . . Mary then in obtaining this Grace for sinners by her intercession, thus restores them to life" (page 73).

"He falls and is LOST who has not recourse to MARY" (page 87).

THE WORD OF GOD:

"For there is one God, and ONE Mediator between God and men, the MAN Christ Jesus" (I Timothy 2:5).

Christ . . . is our life" (Colossians 3:4).

"Wherefore HE is able also to save them to the uttermost that come unto God by HIM, seeing he ever liveth to make intercession for us" (Hebrews 7:25).

"Jesus saith unto him: I am the way, the truth, and the life: no man cometh unto the Father, but by me" (John 14:6).

Mary Is Glorified More Than Jesus Christ

THE ROMAN CATHOLIC CHURCH:

"We shall be heard more quickly . . . if we have recourse to Mary and call on HER holy name, than we should be if we called on the Name of Jesus our Saviour" (page 133).

THE WORD OF GOD:

"In the name of Jesus Christ . . . For there is none OTHER name under heaven given among men, whereby we must be saved" (Acts 3:6; 4:12).

"The holy Church commands a WORSHIP peculiar to MARY" (page 127).

"Many things . . . are asked from God and are not granted; they are asked from MARY and should be obtained," for "she . . . is even Queen of Hell, and Sovereign Mistress of the Devils" (pages 134, 140).

"above . . . every name" (Ephesians 1:21).

"For the Father seeketh such to ADORE HIM" (John 4:23-24).

"Seeing then . . . JESUS the Son of God . . . let us therefore come boldly to the throne of grace: that we may obtain mercy, and find grace" (Hebrews 4:14-16).

Mary is the Gate to Heaven Instead of Jesus Christ

THE ROMAN CATHOLIC CHURCH:

"Mary is called . . . the gate of Heaven because no one can enter that blessed Kingdom without passing through Her" (page 157).

"The way of salvation is open to none otherwise than through MARY. Our salvation is in the hands of Mary . . . he who is protected by MARY will be saved, he who is not will be lost" (pages 167, 168).

THE WORD OF GOD:

"I am the door: by me, if any man enter in, he shall be SAVED . . . " says Christ (John 10:1, 7, 9).

"Jesus saith unto him, I am the way . . . no man cometh unto the Father, but by ME"; "neither is there SALVATION in any other" (John 14:6 and Acts 4:12).

"For the SON of man is come to save that which was lost" (Luke 19:10).

Mary is Given the Power of Jesus Christ

THE ROMAN CATHOLIC CHURCH:

"All power is given to THEE in Heaven and on earth" so that "at the command of MARY all obey—even God . . . and thus . . . God has placed the whole Church . . . under the dominion of MARY" (pages 178, 179).

"O wonderful mercy of our God who . . . has given us His own Mother . . . to be our Advocate." And she "is also the

THE WORD OF GOD:

"ALL POWER is given unto ME in heaven and in earth," so that "at the name of JESUS every knee should bow," "that in all things HE might have the preeminence" (Matthew 28:18; Philippians 2:9-11; Colossians 1:18).

"My little children, these things write I unto you, that ye sin not. And if any man sin, we have an ADVOCATE with

Advocate of the whole human race . . . for SHE can do what SHE wills with God" (pages 187, 192, 197).

the Father, JESUS CHRIST the righteous: and HE is the propitiation for our sins: and not for ours only, but also for the sins of the WHOLE world" (I John 2:1-2).

Mary is the Peacemaker Instead of Jesus Christ Our Peace

THE ROMAN CATHOLIC CHURCH:

"MARY is the Peacemaker between sinners and God." Mary says, "I have been appointed by my Lord THE Peacemaker between sinners and God."

Thus, "Mary . . . is the GREAT Peacemaker, who finds and obtains the reconciliation of enemies with God" (pages 199, 201).

"We often more quickly obtain what we ask by calling on the name of MARY, than by invoking that of Jesus," for "She . . . is our Hope, our Counsel, our Refuge, our Help" (pages 259, 260, 262).

THE WORD OF GOD:

"But now in CHRIST JESUS ye who sometimes were far off are made nigh by the blood of Christ. FOR HE IS OUR PEACE." "Having made peace through the blood of his cross, whether there be things in earth, or things in heaven" (Ephesians 2: 13-14; Colossians 1:20).

"Hitherto have ye asked nothing in MY *name*. ASK, and ye shall receive . . . " for "if we ask anything according to his Will, HE heareth us"; hence "he that believeth not God hath made HIM *a liar*" (John 16:24; I John 5:9-15).

Mary is Given the Glory That Alone Belongs to Jesus Christ

THE ROMAN CATHOLIC CHURCH:

"MARY . . . is that Throne of Grace to which the Apostle Paul, in his Epistle to the Hebrews, exhorts us to fly with confidence . . . " (page 262).

"The whole Trinity, O MARY, gave thee a name . . . above every name, that in THY name, every knee should bow of things in Heaven, on earth and under the earth" (page 265).

THE WORD OF GOD:

"Seeing then . . . JESUS the Son of God" as our "confidence" to "the throne of grace" (Hebrews 4:14-16).

"God also hath highly exalted HIM and given him a name which is above every name: that at the name of JESUS every knee should bow, of things in heaven, and things in earth, and things under the earth; and that every tongue should confess that Jesus Christ is Lord, to the glory of God the Father" (Philippians 2:9-12).

The Catholic Church maintains that she does not encourage the reading of the Scripture lest it be abused. The reader can judge for himself who has abused the Scripture—the subjects of the Catholic Church or its heads.

St. Peter said of false teachers: "But there were false prophets also among the people, even as there shall be false teachers among you, who privily shall bring in damnable heresies, even denying the Lord that brought them, and bring upon themselves swift destruction. And many shall follow their pernicious ways by reason of whom the way of truth shall be evil spoken of. And through covetousness shall they with feigned words make merchandise of you: whose judgment now of a long time lingereth not, and their damnation slumbereth not" (II Peter 2:1-3).

Recently I read of a Catholic priest who was converted; listen to him tell of his devotion to Mary. The following is taken from a little pamphlet called "The Gift":

"In Montreal there is a splendid cathedral, capable of holding 15,000 people. I used to preach there very often. One day the Bishop asked me to speak on the Virgin Mary, and I was glad to do so. I said to those people what I thought to be true then, and what the priests believe and preach everywhere.

'My dear friends, when a man has rebelled against his king, when he has committed a great crime against his emperor, does he come himself to speak to him? If he has a favor to ask from his king, does he dare, under the circumstances, to appear in the king's presence? No; the king would rebuke him, and would punish him. Then, what does he do? Instead of going himself, he selects one

of the friends of the king, some one of his officers, sometimes the sister or the mother of the king, and he puts his
petition into their hands. This person speaks in favor
of the guilty man. He asks the king's pardon, appeases
his wrath, and very often the king will grant to this person the favor which he would refuse to the guilty man.

'Then,' I said, 'we are all sinners, we have all offended
the great and mighty king, the King of kings. We have
raised rebellious colors against Him. We have trampled
His laws under our feet, and surely He is angry with us.
What can we do today? Shall we go ourselves with our
hands filled with our iniquities? No! But, thanks to God,
we have Mary the mother of Jesus, our King, at His right
hand, and as a dutiful son never refuses any favor to a
beloved mother, so Jesus will never refuse any favor to
Mary. He has never refused any petition which she presented to Him when He was on earth. He has never rebuked His mother in any way. Where is the son who
would break the heart of a loving mother, when he could
rejoice her by granting her what she wants? Then I say,
Jesus the King of kings, is not only the Son of God, but
He is the Son of Mary, and He loves His mother. As He
has never refused any favor to Mary when He was on
earth, so He will never refuse her any favor today. Then
what must we do? Oh! We cannot present ourselves before the great King, covered as we are with iniquity. Let
us present our petitions to His holy mother; she will go to
the feet of Jesus herself; from Jesus, her God and her
son, she will surely receive the favors which she will ask;
she will ask your pardon and will obtain it. She will
ask a place in the kingdom of Christ, and you will have
it. She will ask Jesus to forget your iniquities, to grant
you the true repentance, and He will give you anything
His mother may ask of Him.'

"My hearers were so happy at the idea of having such
an advocate at the feet of Jesus interceding for them day

and night, that they all burst into tears, and were beside themselves with joy that Mary was to ask and obtain their pardon.

"I thought, at the time, that this was not only the religion of Christ but that it was the religion of common sense, and that nothing could be said against it. After the sermon the Bishop came to me and blessed me, and thanked me, saying that the sermon would do great good in Montreal.

"That night I went on my knees, and took my Bible, and my heart was full of joy because of the good sermon I had given in the morning. I opened and read from Matthew 12:46-50, the following words: 'While he yet talked to the people, behold, his mother and his brethren stood without, desiring to speak with him. Then one said unto him, Behold thy mother and thy brethren stand without desiring to speak with thee. But he answered and said to him that told him, Who is my mother? and who are my brethren? And he stretched forth his hand toward his disciples and said, Behold my mother and my brethren for whosoever shall do the will of my father which is in heaven, the same is my brother, and sister, and mother.'

"When I had read these words there was a voice speaking to me more terrible than the voice of loud thunder, saying, 'Chiniquy, you preached a lie this morning when you said that Mary had always received the favors which she had asked from Jesus. Do you not see that Mary comes to ask a favor, that is, to see her son, during whose absence she has been lonesome, and who has left her during many months to preach the Gospel?' When Mary gets to the place where Jesus is preaching, the place is so crammed that she cannot enter. What will she do? She will do what every mother would do in her place. She raises her voice and requests Him to come and see her; but while Jesus hears the voice of His mother, and with His divine eyes sees her, does He grant her petition?

No. He shuts His ears to her voice and hardens His heart against her prayer. It is a public rebuke, and she feels it keenly. The people are astonished. They are puzzled, almost scandalized. They turn to Christ, and they say to Him, 'Why don't you come and speak to your mother?' What does Jesus say? He gives no answer except this extraordinary one: 'Who is my mother? and who are my brethren?' and, looking upon His disciples, He says: 'Behold my mother, my brethren, and my sisters.' As for Mary, she is left alone, and publicly rebuked.

"And then the voice spoke to me again with the power of thunder, telling me to read again in Mark 3:31-35. You will find that Mark says that Jesus 'rebuked' His mother. Read Luke 8:19-21. Luke says that Jesus 'rebuked' His mother. He would not grant the petition. And then the voice spoke to me with terrible power, telling me that Jesus, so long as He was a little boy, obeyed His father and His mother; but as soon as Jesus presented Himself before the world as the Son of God, as the Saviour of the world, as the great Light of humanity, then Mary had to disappear. It is to Jesus alone that the eyes of the world must be turned to receive Light and Life.

"Then, my friends, the voice spoke to me all the night: 'Chiniquy, Chiniquy, you have said a lie this morning, and you were preaching a lot of fables and nonsense; and you preach against the Scriptures when you say that Mary has the power to grant any favor from Jesus.' I prayed and I wept, and it was a sleepless night with me.

"The next morning I went to table with the Bishop-Prince, the coadjutor, who had invited me to breakfast. He said to me, 'Mr. Chiniquy, you look like a man who has spent the night in tears. What is the matter with you?' I said, 'My lord, you are correct. I am desolate above measure.' 'What is the matter?' he said. 'Oh! I cannot say here,' I said. 'Will you please give me one hour in

your room alone? I will tell you a mystery which will
puzzle you.'

"After breakfast I went out with him and said, 'Yesterday you paid me great compliments because of the sermon
where I proved that Jesus had always granted the
petitions of His mother; but, my lord, last night I heard
another voice, stronger than yours, and my desolation is
that I believe that voice is the voice of God. That voice
has told me that we Roman Catholic priests and bishops
preach a blasphemous falsehood every time we say to the
people that Mary has always the power to receive from
the hands of Jesus Christ the favors which she asks. This
is a lie, my lord—this, I fear, is a diabolical and damning
error.'

"The Bishop then said, 'Mr. Chiniquy, what do you
mean? Are you a Protestant?' 'No,' I said, 'I am not a
Protestant.' (Many times I had been called a Protestant
because I was so fond of the Bible.) 'But I tell you in your
face that I sincerely fear that yesterday I preached a lie,
and that you, my lord, will preach one also the next time
you say that we must invoke Mary, under the pretext that
Jesus has never refused any favor to His mother. This
is false.'

"The Bishop said, 'Mr. Chiniquy, you go too far!'

" 'No, my lord,' I said, 'it is of no use to talk. Here is the
Gospel; read it.' And I put the Gospel into the hands of
the Bishop, and he read with his own eyes what I have
already quoted. My impression was that he read those
words for the first time. The poor man was so much
surprised that he remained mute and trembling. Finally
he asked, 'What does that mean?'

" 'Well,' I said, 'this is the Gospel; and here you see that
Mary has come to ask from Jesus Christ a favor, and He
has not only rebuked her, but has refused to consider her
as His mother. He did this publicly, that we might know

that Mary is the mother of Jesus as man, and not as God.'
The Bishop was beside himself. He could not answer me.

"I then asked to be allowed to put to him a few questions. I said, 'My lord, who has saved you and saved me upon the Cross?' He answered, 'Jesus Christ.' 'And who paid your debts and mine by shedding His blood; was it Mary or Jesus?' He said, 'Jesus Christ.'

" 'Now, my lord, when Jesus and Mary were on earth, who loved the sinner more; was it Mary or Jesus? Did any sinner come to Mary on earth to be saved?'

" 'No.'

" 'Do you remember that any sinner has gone to Jesus to be saved?'

" 'Yes, many.'

" 'Have they been rebuked?'

" 'Never.'

" 'Do you remember that Jesus said sometimes, to sinners, Come to Mary and she will save you?'

" 'No,' he said. 'Do you remember that Jesus has said to the poor sinners, Come unto me?'

" 'Yes, He has said it.'

" 'Has He ever retracted those words?'

" 'No!'

" 'And who was, then, the more powerful to save sinners?' I asked. 'Oh! it was Jesus!'

" 'Now, my lord, since Jesus and Mary are now in heaven, can you show me in the Scripture that Jesus has lost anything of His desire and power to save sinners, or that what He has lost has been gained by Mary? And the Bishop answered, 'No.'

" 'Then, my lord,' I asked, 'why do we not go to Him, and Him alone? Why do we invite poor sinners to come to Mary, when, by your own confession, she is nothing compared with Jesus, in power, in mercy, in love and in compassion for the sinner?'

"Then the poor Bishop was like a man who is condemned to death. He trembled before me, and as he could not answer me, he pleaded business and left me. His 'business' was that he could not answer me."

Father Chiniquy, whose testimony you have just read, saw the truth of the Word of God—that to become a Christian one must believe on the Lord Jesus Christ and trust in Him alone for salvation, apart from anything else, even Mary. He then became a preacher of the pure Gospel of Grace, rather than a priest dictating the doctrines of Rome.

Oh, dear reader, if you are not a Christian, cannot you see that it is Jesus who paid the penalty for your sin, and that it is He who can and will save you? Romans 4:5: "But to him that worketh not, but believeth on him that justifieth the ungodly, his faith is counted for righteousness." Ephesians 2:8-9: "For by grace are ye saved through faith; and that not of yourselves: it is the gift of God: not of works, lest any man should boast."

Can you say with the redeemed of the Lord:

> "My hope is built on nothing less
> Than Jesus' Blood and Righteousness"?

To the educator Jesus is the great Teacher (John 3:2).

To the farmer He is the Sower and Lord of harvest (Luke 10:2).

To the artist He is the one altogether lovely (Song of Solomon 5:16).

To the architect He is the chief Corner stone (I Peter 2:6).

To the builder He is the sure Foundation (Isaiah 28:16).

To the carpenter He is the Door (John 10:7).

To the banker He is the hidden Treasure (Matthew 13:44).

To the engineer He is the new and living Way (Hebrews 10:20).

To the doctor He is the great Physician (Jeremiah 8:22).

To the baker He is the Bread of life (John 6:35).

To the astronomer He is the Sun of righteousness (Malachi 4:2).

To the florist He is the Rose of Sharon (Song of Solomon 2:1).

To the geologist He is the Rock of Ages (I Cor. 10:4).

To the horticulturist He is the true Vine (John 15:1).

To the judge He is the only righteous Judge of man (II Tim. 4:8).

To the juror He is the faithful and true Witness (Rev. 3:14).

To the jeweler He is the Pearl of great price (Matthew 13:46).

To the lawyer He is Counsellor, Lawgiver and true Advocate (Isaiah 9:6).

To the newspaper man He is Tidings of great joy (Luke 2:10).

To the oculist He is the Light of the eyes (Proverbs 29:13).

To the philanthropist He is the unspeakable Gift (II Cor. 9:15).

To the philosopher He is the Wisdom of God (I Cor. 1:24).

To the preacher He is the Word of God (Revelation 19:13).

To the sculptor He is the living Stone (I Peter 2:4).

To the servant He is the good Master (Matthew 23:8-10).

To the statesman He is the Desire of all Nations (Haggai 2:7).

To the student He is the incarnate Truth (I John 5:6).

To the theologian He is the Author and Finisher of our faith (Hebrews 12:2).

To the toiler He is the Giver of rest (Matthew 11:28).

To the sinner He is the Lamb of God who takes sin away (John 1:29).

To the Christian He is the Son of the living God, the Saviour, the Redeemer and the loving God.

Someone has said: "To many Jesus is only a grand subject for a painting, a heroic theme for a pen, a beautiful form for a statue and a thought for a song; but to those who have heard His voice, who have felt His pardon, who have received His benediction, He is music, warmth, light, joy, hope and salvation, a Friend that never forsakes, lifting you up when others try to push you down. We cannot wear Him out; we pile on Him all our griefs and troubles; yet He is always ready to lift us up; He is always ready to help us. He addresses us with the same love; He beams down upon us with the same compassion. There is no name like His. It is more inspirational than Caesar's; it is more musical than Beethoven's; it is more conquering than Napoleon's; it is more eloquent than Demosthenes'; it is more inspiring than Washington's; it is more patient than Lincoln's.

"The name of Jesus throbs with all life; it weeps with all pathos; it groans with all pain; it stoops with all love; its breath is laden with perfume. Who like Jesus can pity a homeless orphan? Who like Jesus can welcome a prodigal back home? Who like Jesus can make a drunkard sober? Who like Jesus can illuminate a cemetery plowed with graves? Who like Jesus can make a queen unto God out of the lost woman of the street? Who like Jesus can kiss away our sorrow? Who like Jesus can mend a broken home? 'Neither is there salvation in any other: for there is none other name under heaven given among men, whereby we must be saved' " (Acts 4:12).

This is one religion of the world in which many of its devotees have not heard of God's love and mercy and His wonderful Word, the Bible, that we love and cherish and for which we would die.

The Roman Catholic Church does not believe that the Virgin Mary was a sinner and does not teach nor believe that she had children. In Rom. 3:23 we read "For all have sinned, and come short of the glory of God." This, of course, means the Virgin Mary also. The Virgin Mary did become Joseph's wife after the birth of Jesus, for we read, "And [Joseph] knew her not till she had brought forth her firstborn son" (Matt. 1:24-25). But he knew her after Christ was born, as the Scriptures say. Furthermore, it is proved that she had children after the birth of Jesus, for in Matt. 13:55-57 we read, "Is not this the carpenter's son? is not his mother called Mary? And his brethren [brothers] James and Joses, and Simon and Judas? And his sisters, are they not all with us?" Here we see very plainly that Jesus had brothers and sisters; and we cannot deny it, for the Word of God says so. In Mark 6:3 we read again the names of the brothers of Jesus and again we read he had sisters. In Gal. 1:19 we read, "But other of the apostles saw I none, save the Lord's brother."

The Bible says that all were born in sin, but there was One who did no sin, neither was guile found in His mouth (I Pet. 2:22). It was because Mary found favor in the sight of the Lord that Jesus was placed in her womb; not because she was sinless, but because she was God-fearing. More prayers are addressed to the Virgin Mary than to any other saint in the Roman Church. More prayers are prayed to her than to God through Jesus' name. Let us examine the Scripture again. We know —I did it thousands of times—that when Roman Catholics pray, they ask God in the name of the Virgin Mary to grant their petitions. The Bible teaches that prayers are to be asked in the name of Jesus Christ (John 14:14)— and not in the name of the Virgin Mary.

Let us sum up everything in a nutshell. The following is taken from a tract by G. M. U. No. 370, which is printed in Anthony Zeoli's tract, "Light for Roman Catholics."

Of the many institutions contrary to the gospel, which are practiced by the Romish Church today, the earliest in origin appeared to be prayers for the dead and the making of the sign of the cross, both of which came into existence about three hundred years after Christ and the Apostles. Notice, these things that we shall now relate have not been from the beginning when Christ came and revealed God's plan to be the penalty of our sins, but the fallacies have been added by men who are sinners, according to the Bible. No man, be he pope, priest, minister, preacher, evangelist, or layman, has the right or power to change the teachings of Christ.

I read in Ps. 89:34 "My covenant will I not break, nor alter the thing that is gone out of my lips." Again, in Ps. 119:89: "Forever, O Lord, thy word is settled in heaven." Sin has never changed; so God's message is the same.

Let us look into the Scriptures—Isa. 40:8: "The grass withereth, the flower fadeth: but the word of our God shall stand forever." Then again, "But the word of the Lord endureth forever. And this is the word which by the gospel [of good tidings] is preached unto you" (I Pet. 1:25). In II Tim. 3:16: "All scripture is given by inspiration of God, and is profitable for doctrine, for reproof, for correction, for instruction in righteousness."

About six hundred years after Christ and the Apostles, Gregory I established a worship in an unknown tongue, or in Latin. The gospel teaches us that our prayers should be addressed to God alone. Prayers were never offered to Mary and the saints by the Apostles and members of the Early Church. The worship of Mary and the saints was commenced about six hundred years after Christ and the Apostles.

The worship of the cross, images and relics was established about seven hundred and eighty-eight years after Christ. It is impossible to find a single trace of this practice in the Gospels.

The baptism of bells does not come from the Bible, Christ, or the Apostles. This baptism was invented nine hundred and sixty-five years after the beginning of the Early Church, by Pope John XIV.

It was about nine hundred and ninety-eight years after the Apostles that Lent was imposed upon the Roman Catholic Church. Lent and the obligatory fast on Friday are commandments of men, not teachings of the gospel.

Holy water, mixed with a pinch of salt and blessed by the priest, was authorized in the year 850. As a Roman Catholic lad often on Saturday I would get to church too early for confession. The priest would request me to fill the holy-water box that rested in the vestibule of the church. People dip their fingers in this water, and as they approach the inside of the church they make the sign of the cross. I would take the box to the sink, fill it with water, and then the priest would mumble some words over it. Then it became holy water, according to the Roman Catholic Church. Surely this cannot be found in Scripture. Remember, we are taking the HOLY SCRIPTURES as our authority, for the true Church is built and stands upon the WORD OF GOD.

Boniface VII is the pope who made the law against the marriage of the priest, ten hundred and seventy-nine years after Christ. The gospel teaches the marriage of the clergy.

The Sacrifice of the Mass is a novelty and has been in existence only since the eleventh century. The gospel teaches us that the SACRIFICE OF CHRIST was offered *once for all*.

About eleven hundred and ninety years after Christ, the Roman Catholic Church began the sale of indulgences. The Christian religion as it is taught in the gospel condemns such a traffic. Again the work of Christ is made of no effect in forgiveness of sin. It was a protest against the traffic that brought on the Protestant Reformation in the sixteenth century.

The Roman Catholic Church uses a wafer in the Lord's Supper instead of bread; this change was made about the time that the doctrine of transubstantiation was proclaimed an article of faith by Pope Innocent III in the year 1215 A.D. In the year 1220, Pope Honorius invented the adoration of this wafer (Host). Thus far we see the Roman Catholics worship a God made by the hands of men. Please do not misunderstand me. I do not hate the Roman Catholic people. I love them. I want to help them, but I fear their system. It is their religious system that I am bringing to light in these pages; oh, that they might sit down and examine these things and see if they are of God or men.

A god made with hands—the adoration of such a god is entirely contrary to the gospel preached by Jesus Christ.

Auricular confession, or confession to the priest, was also instituted by Pope Innocent III during the session of the Council of Lateran, twelve hundred and fifteen years after Christ.

Since the year 1414 the Roman Catholic Church has refused to give the cup of wine to the people in the Communion service. This institution of Christ was changed by the Council of Constance. The gospel teaches that the Lord's Supper should be given with bread and wine.

Purgatory was proclaimed an article of faith fourteen hundred and thirty-eight years after the Apostles by the Council of Florence. The writers of the Gospels do not give one Scripture or word that speaks about the Roman Catholic purgatory.

Roman Catholic traditions were placed on the same level with the Holy Scriptures by the Council of Trent fifteen hundred and forty-five years after Christ. These traditions are simply teachings of men.

The Apocryphal books, some doubtless false, and none of them inspired, were placed in the Bible by the Council of Trent fifteen hundred and forty-six years after the Apostles.

Eighteen hundred and fifty-four years after Christ the Roman Catholic Church invented the doctrine that Mary was born without sin, but the gospel teaches all have sinned. The gospel teaches that there is not a man upon the earth that doeth good and sinneth not (Prov. 20:9; Rom. 3:23).

CHAPTER VIII

MARRIAGE

Now we come to the subject of "marriage." The Roman Catholic Church forbids her clergy to marry, and according to God's Word this doctrine is error. In I Timothy 4 we read, "Some shall depart from the faith, giving heed to spirits of error and doctrines of devils" (I Tim. 4:1). . . . "Forbidding to marry" (I Tim. 4:3). These are very plain statements taken from the Roman Catholic Bible, and as these verses mean just what they say, Roman Catholicism is in error because it forbids its clergy to marry.

It was Pope Gregory VII who said, "Leave your wives, children and homes and follow me. My clergy shall not marry." This pope, we know, was not Peter's successor, and therefore he practiced such wickedness. The Roman Catholic priests and nuns cannot marry, according to the Roman Catholic religion, in spite of the fact that the Roman Catholic Bible says that any religion forbidding marriage is a doctrine of devils and error.

I am trying to show the reader how far away from the teachings of Christ the Roman Catholic Church has gone. So how can she claim to be the true Church when she has departed from the teachings and practices of the Bible and the Early Church? I am not trying to expose the faults of any individual, but the practices of a system that is far removed from God and the plain teachings of the Word.

The Catholic Church says that popes cannot marry. It declares that Peter was the first pope; but the Bible states clearly that he was a married man. One of Christ's miracles was performed when he raised Peter's wife's mother who lay sick with a fever. Some priests say that when Peter became pope he left his wife. Do they mean to say, then, that their church is built upon a wife deserter?

I feel that I should strike a note of warning here. People ask: "If this is all true, how does Rome make her converts?" She does not have Bible study, prayermeetings, evangelistic meetings; how then does she make converts? As a Roman Catholic for sixteen years, and one that desired to be a priest, let me tell you how it is done. In many Roman churches they have what is called the preaching mission, where once a year a priest will hold two weeks' meetings, throwing them open to Protestants as well as Catholics. Many times I attended this mission, sitting at the feet of a special priest. These were his words: "When you men are thinking about getting married, try if at all possible to choose a Protestant girl; do not marry her unless she promises that she will be married by the priest and that she will turn to the Roman Church and rear her children as Roman Catholics." The next night would be for young girls only, when the same advice would be given with these words: "When he proposes to you promise him you will marry him only if he turns Roman Catholic and is married by the priest and will rear the children as Roman Catholic. Only then will I marry you." This is how Rome works.

Christian young men and women should not pick their mates from the Roman Church or any other religion, for the Bible says, "Be ye not unequally yoked together" (II Cor. 6:14). O young men and women, do you know Christ as your personal Saviour? If you do, walk ye in His steps. Live close to Him at all times.

For a few moments you have been sitting with me on the sidelines as I took you into the Roman Church and let you see its teaching and practices of today. I know what your conclusions are. The Roman Church is a church made up of the doctrines and ideas of men. Hallelujah for the Word of God, for the shield, light, hope, faith, that come by reading its pages!

We therefore see, dear friend, that the Roman Catholic Church does not teach her people what the Roman Catholic Bible teaches, nor does she practice the teachings of this Bible.

CHAPTER IX

THE BIBLE

THE purpose of the following paragraphs is to give a clearer understanding of what the Catholic Church teaches and to view these teachings in the light of the Holy Scriptures. I desire to prove to the reader that much of what the Catholic Church teaches about the Bible is in direct contradiction to the teachings of Christ as given to us in the Holy Bible, including the Douay Version. This is written to reveal her teachings to lukewarm Christians, indifferent Christians who have Catholic sympathties, and others who desire light on the teachings of Catholicism. I desire to quote from a thirty-six page pamphlet approved by Catholic authorities and published by the Paulist Press, New York; it is entitled "What the Catholic Church Is; And What She Teaches," by Rev. E. R. Hull S.J. This pamphlet is so cleverly worded in defense of Catholic doctrine to non-Catholic that it makes light of Christian teaching and everything that dares to rise above the Catholic Church. I quote from page 2:

"The Catholic Church considers that the Bible was never intended for the sole and adequate rule of faith, partly because it is not a sufficiently exhaustive account of all Christian teaching, and partly because its expressions of doctrine are often ambiguous and require authoritative interpretation. The New Testament does not bear the marks of having been drawn up to serve as a code of Christian belief. Neither does it direct us to take the Scripture as our sole rule of faith, or free us from the obligation of believing more than is clearly taught in the Scriptures."

How clever to minimize the Scripture so that a church or group of people can attach so much rubbish to it! If the above is true, then the Scripture cannot be trusted. But, God's Word says in Romans 3:4: "Let God be true, but every man a liar." Please turn with me to II Timothy 3:16 where we read the following: "All scripture is given by inspiration of God, and is profitable for doctrine, for reproof, for correction, for instruction in righteousness." Now, according to this, on what authority can anyone minimize the Scripture? We as Christians and followers of Christ feel and know from studying the Scripture that the Bible is accepted as the very Word of God and is recognized as the sole and adequate rule of faith.

We are told in the Bible to search the Scripture, to study it, to be hearers of it, and also to be doers of the Word (John 5:39; James 1:22; II Timothy 2:15).

The Bible (above any authority) is to the Christian the prize possession of his life. Study its philosophy, its prophecies, its judiciary, its astronomy, its histories, its entire message, and you will find that it leads and points to Christ as the Saviour of the world—never to a church.

The Bible gives light, wisdom, understanding and courage to those who have accepted it as the Word of God, and taken Christ Jesus as their personal Saviour (John 9:4-5; II Tim. 2:15). To the person who rejects the Word of God and feels he must trust in something else, apart from the Scriptures, I will quote John 8:47: "He that is of God heareth God's words: ye therefore hear them not, because ye are not of God." The Scripture is God's word—not the church. Our faith, hope and trust should be in the written Word (the Bible). Only then can we come to know Christ who is the Living Word.

The Bible should be to every one the sole rule of faith, apart from any institution or church built by men. The Bible is the Word of God, and faith cometh by hearing— hearing the Word of God (Rom. 10:17). Notice: not the *word of the church*, but the *Word of God*.

I believe the Bible to be the Word of God because of the unity of the books, because of its fulfilled prophecy, because of its superiority to other books, because of its power to lift men up to God, because of the character of those who accept it, because of its unexhaustible depths and because of the fact that as one grows in knowledge and character, wisdom and holiness, one grows towards the Bible. The more I commune with God in prayer, the more precious His Word (the Bible) becomes.

Study the biography of the Bible, and you will find Christ as the Life and Light of men (John 1:1-5; I John 1:5). Study the history of the Bible, and you will find Christ is the Beginning and the End (Rev. 22:13). Study the geology of the Bible, and you will find Christ as the Rock of Ages. Study the husbandry of the Bible, and you will find Christ as the chief Corner stone. Study the carpentry of the Bible, and you will find Christ as the open Door (John 10:9). Study the botany of the Bible, and you will find Christ as the Lily of the valley (Song of Solomon 2:1). Study the therapy of the Bible, and you will find Christ as the great Physician. Study the judiciary of the Bible, and you will find Christ as the righteous Judge. Study the astronomy of the Bible, and you will find Christ as the Bright and Morning Star. Study the biology of the Bible, and you will find Christ as the Lamb of God (John 1:29). Study the philosophy of the Bible, and you will find that only a fool saith in his heart that there is no God and that the Bible is not the Word of God. Grasp the message of the Bible, and you will find that all men are sinners lost and condemned, but God in His great love sent Christ to pay the penalty for our sins, that we, through accepting Him, might be saved.

God's Word is sufficient and complete without additions by any church or other organization.

"All scripture is given by inspiration of God" (II Timothy 3:16).

The late Dr. John Roach Straton once said: "The Bible is a glorious temple of truth, with its broad foundations in Genesis, its majestic columns rising in the record of patriarch, prophet and priest, its roof-tree in the Gospels of Jesus Christ and its majestic dome in the Revelation of a New Heaven and New Earth wherein will dwell righteousness."

The Bible declares itself to be inspired in a unique sense. It professes to be an authoritative message from God. It says, "Holy men of God spake as they were moved by the Holy Ghost."

More than a thousand times, the writers of the sacred manuscripts said distinctly that they were writing God's words—namely, that they were supernaturally inspired to write. I do not believe that such men as Moses, Isaiah, Paul and John were self-deceived. When they said they were recording the words of God, they were recording the words of God! Being dependable, trustworthy men, they told the truth.

> Whence but from heaven could men unskilled in arts,
> In several ages, born in several parts,
> Weave such agreeing truths? Or how or why
> Should all conspire to cheat us with a lie?
> Unasked their pains, ungrateful their advice,
> Starving their gains, and martyrdom their price.

Christ came to the earth and showed by His life, teaching and miracles that He was what He claimed to be— the Eternal Son of God. And, during the days of His flesh, He accepted the Old Testament Scriptures as supernaturally inspired. Speaking with finality, He said: "For verily I say unto you, Till heaven and earth pass, one jot or one tittle shall in no wise pass from the law, till all be fulfilled."

If you make the mistake of rejecting the deity of Christ, accepting the lower view, that He was only the wisest and best of men, still His word is worth more than that of any other man. If I close my mind to the testimony of men, as to the inspiration of the Bible, I will accept what He says as true.

THE WORD STANDS

Now no one can deny that the Bible is here. It is an objective reality and not a subjective idea. Here it is! You may hold a copy in your hand. The Book has not only existed for thousands of years, but has survived all efforts to destroy it. Not only has it been subjected to the vicissitudes of fortune and the catastrophes of history that have destroyed other valuable books, which were former treasures of the human race, but calculated and definite steps have been taken from time to time to wipe it utterly from the earth.

Toustal bought and burned the whole of Tyndale's first edition, but failed to destroy the Book or prevent its circulation. Tyndale took the money and with it printed a far larger edition, and the Bibles were shipped into Old England wrapped in bales of cloth, barrels and kegs and even coffins used as packing cases. It is said that in one century 150,000 people were butchered for reading the Bible. The jailer's key, the headman's ax, the rope of the gallows, the fagot of the bigot, the powder of the poisoner, the dagger of the assassin have all combined in the effort to annihilate it.

This Book has successfully resisted the sophistries of Hume, the misguided eloquence of Gibbon, the rationalism of Rousseau, the ignorant blasphemies of Thomas Paine, the satirical mockery of Voltaire, the idle quibbling of Strauss, the shallow witticisms of Renan, the cheap buffoonery of Bob Ingersoll, the audacious assaults of the revolutionists of France and the insidious duplicity of the rationalistic theologians of Germany. It has also resisted the foolish claims of the Roman Catholic system.

As with Moses' bush, the Bible has burned, but it has not been consumed. Phoenix-like, it has risen from its ashes to new heights of usefulness and power.

It is inconceivable that a loving Heavenly Father would leave His offspring without a message. Such a thing is as difficult for me to believe as to believe that kind and loving parents would bring children into this world and not communicate with them. Offspring might refuse to listen and reject admonition, but it would nevertheless be natural for parents to try to teach them.

God has not cast off free moral agents, created in His own image, even if that image was later distorted by sin. He has given them an authoritative revelation that explains the mysteries of life and death, the here and the hereafter.

INTERNAL EVIDENCE

The Bible is in reality a library made up of sixty-six books, written by about forty different authors during a period of fifteen hundred years. Some of these writers were widely separated by time and distance, and came from different walks of life; they were prophets, priests, shepherds, farmers, fishermen, statesmen and kings. They all maintained that the product of their pens was from God.

An examination of these sixty-six books reveals that they are one Book. They comprise a perfect unit in design and arrangement. Each breathes the same wonderful message of salvation from sin. There are no contradictions or conflicts. They blend into one another like different parts of a mechanism, produced by a master mechanic. This Book was given as the sole rule of faith: "These are written, that ye might believe that Jesus is the Christ, the Son of God; and that believing ye might have life through his name" (John 20:31).

II Tim. 4:1-4 says, "I charge thee therefore before God, and the Lord Jesus Christ, who shall judge the quick and the dead at his appearing and his kingdom: *Preach the word; be instant in season, out of season; reprove, rebuke, exhort with all longsuffering and doctrine.* For the time will come when they will not endure sound doctrine; but after their own lusts shall they heap to themselves teachers, having itching ears. And they shall turn away their ears from the truth, and shall be turned unto FABLES."

God's Word says, "For I testify unto every man that heareth the words of the prophecy of this book, If any man shall add unto these things, God shall add unto him the plagues that are written in this book: And if any man shall take away from the words of the book of this prophecy, God shall take away his part out of the book of life, and out of the holy city, and from the things which are written in this book" (Rev. 22:18-19).

The Apostle Paul says in Gal. 1:8: "But though we, or an angel from heaven, preach any other gospel unto you than that which we have preached unto you, let him be accursed."

What right or authority has man to change the Christian teachings and doctrine given to the world by Jesus Christ? No authority whatever. The Word of God does not need changing. It is sure and firm. Of men who change it we are told, "Let him be accursed."

We read in Mal. 2:1-3: "And now, O ye priests, this commandment is for you. If ye will not hear, and if ye will not lay it to heart, to give glory unto my name, saith the Lord of hosts, I will even send a curse upon you, and I will curse your blessings: yea, I have cursed them already, because ye do not lay it to heart. Behold, I will corrupt your seed, and spread dung upon your faces, even the dung of your solemn feasts; and one shall take you away with it."

Friends, the Protestant Church does not save, nor does the Romish Church, *but,* hallelujah, He, Jesus Christ, who died for my sins, to Him I may go. So then, dear reader, if you have never received Jesus as your personal Saviour, do it right now.

His Word says, "But as many as received him, to them gave he power to become the sons of God, even to them that believe on his name."

"Today if ye will hear his voice, harden not your hearts, as in the provocation" (Heb. 3:15).

In Isa. 1:18 God says, "Come now, and let us reason together, saith the Lord: though your sins be as scarlet, they shall be as white as snow; though they be red like crimson, they shall be as wool."

I plead with you, dear reader, will you not now receive Him (Jesus) as your personal Saviour? Ask Him to come into your heart and life, as you look by faith to the cross and see the Lamb of God hanging there for you. Oh, how He loves you and pleads that you may come to Him. Will you not trust Him now?

"Choose ye this day whom ye will serve" (Josh. 24: 15).

You ask, "What must I do to be saved?" I answer, "Believe on the Lord Jesus Christ, and thou shalt be saved" (Acts 16:31). Receive Him now and be made free for time and eternity.

In the first part of this message we gave you a Scriptural exposition of the true Church. We met the false assertions of Catholicism by revealing to you its teachings and practices, showing that these are not of the true Church, but of a church made by the hands of men.

O Lord, open Thou our eyes; show us Thy truth and Thy way. O God, lead us not in the way man would teach us, but have us go the way Thy Word teaches us and show us the way we are to go. O God, deliver us from man's teachings and guesses and ways; lead us out into Thy way.

My prayer is that these words will not harden your heart but soften your heart and point you to the way of

Christ that through Him many souls may be led from darkness into light.

Will you say it to Him just now? He wants to come into your life. His blood was shed for you; His body was broken for you. He is our sin-bearer. He is our Mediator, and since He is, let us come to Him. "For there is one God, and one mediator between God and man, the man, Christ Jesus."

> Just as I am, without one plea,
> But that Thy blood was shed for me;
> And that Thou bidd'st me come to Thee,
> O Lamb of God, I come! I come!

For the benefit of those who are still skeptical of what I have been saying, may I say to my Roman Catholic friends:

1. Nowhere in the New Testament does Jesus Christ give the Roman Church any power or authority or privilege or rights or distinction over other churches.

2. Nowhere does He authorize any man to be a successor of St. Peter or to be the vicar of Christ or to be pope or to exercise the functions or powers claimed by your pope.

3. Nowhere does He authorize the office of cardinal as claimed by the Roman Church; neither do your own Scriptures authorize your pope, or cardinals, or bishops, or priests, to establish such a thing as your confessional, or to hear confession of sin and to absolve from sin or forgive sins.

4. Nowhere does He authorize people to pray to Mary or to pray to saints.

5. Nowhere in your own Scriptures does He authorize the Roman Catholic "Mass." Nowhere does He authorize the use of holy water or command abstinence from the use of meats on Friday or approve of the use of images in

the church or the cure of sickness by the use of dead men's bones.

6. Nowhere does He give any priest or any other Roman Catholic functionary the power to pray people out of purgatory.

7. Nowhere does He authorize the building up of nunneries and monasteries.

All of these practices are without the slightest authority in the New Testament or in any part of the Word of God, and they are all absolutely repugnant to the teachings of Jesus Christ.

Every one of these things has its roots in ancient heathenism, but they cannot be found in Christianity. This is why I continue to shout aloud, in love, that your practices in the Roman Catholic Church are drawn more from heathenism than from Christianity, and that the Roman Catholic Church as we see it today can scarcely claim to be a Christian church at all.

The whole system from top to bottom, from pope to priest, is built on false assertions. It is deceptive and most misleading to its devotees. It is without divine sanction; it is a fraud on humanity.

If you can find a passage in the New Testament to authorize the things I have named as false, please give me chapter and verse. I do not lay any accusation against you, my Roman Catholic friends, as I love you and want your souls saved; but I cannot approve of your system.

It is only by the grace of God—through faith in Christ, and not one's good works—that salvation comes. Good works are the result of saving faith. Our good works cannot merit salvation. Those who try to be saved by their good works have fallen from the grace of God and have no part in the salvation wrought by Christ.

Purgatory is a libel on the efficacy of the blood of Christ, which cleanseth us from all sin. It would make

God unjust by allowing only those who can pay for masses to get out of it.

In the New Testament, all believers in Christ on earth are called saints. They became saints by their conversion. Their names are written in heaven, and they would be the first to reject worship of themselves.

The Roman Catholic Church is the only church that has altered the Holy Sacrament, and since 1414 it has denied the people the cup. Jesus used bread and wine to represent His body and blood. It was to be a memorial of His death and in remembrance of Him until He comes again. For centuries the Communion was given to the people as well as the clergy, even in the Roman Catholic Church. It is given in the Greek Orthodox and Protestant evangelical churches to this day—only the Roman Catholic Church has changed the Sacrament.

The Virgin Mary is duly respected and honored in all churches, but she was saved as we are. She believed the Word of God and accepted God's message. She left the religion in which she was born and was a convert, and gave her testimony in the Magnificat. She took part in prayer-meetings with the Apostles, received the Holy Ghost at Pentecost and was in the meeting where three thousand were converted. She was a model Christian. She would be the first one to protest against praying to her or honoring her with pagan festivals.

Bishops, pastors and elders are allowed in the New Testament, but not as sacrificers at the altar. Christ is the only High Priest who lives forever. His sacrifice cannot be repeated. The clergy are not masters of the people, but preachers and servants. According to St. Paul, they should be married.

Confession of sin is recommended all through the Bible, but always to God. All good Christians confess their sins to God every day at eventide. Public confession is still practiced in some testimony-meetings.

The title of "pope" was refused by many holy bishops in the early centuries of the Church and was first given to the Bishop of Rome in 610 by the wicked Emperor Phocas.

Peter never was a Roman Catholic. He was converted, or brought to Christ, by his brother Andrew—first a convert, then a disciple and later an Apostle. He made the first confession that Jesus is the Christ, the Son of the living God, and Jesus made this declaration the foundation of His Church. He sinned many, many times and confessed directly to Jesus. He was a plain open-air preacher and an elder. He preached mostly to the Jews and was never in Rome, according to the Bible. He preached the gospel of Christ fearlessly, saying that Jesus Christ alone is the Head of the Church and the only name under heaven whereby we must be saved. He also advised the reading of the Scriptures.

Now, let me summarize. The Lord Jesus Christ founded His Church. He was to be the Head, the Holy Spirit, the Guide, and the Bible was to be the only rule. The Church was composed of His followers, who were born again and pledged to continue His work in the world. It was catholic in that it was designed for all the people of the earth. The Church remained faithful to the gospel for three hundred years, and that was the age of martyrs, persecuted by pagan Rome. After the conversion of Constantine (310 A.D.) Christianity was the State religion, and many pagans were admitted to the Church by baptism without being born again. They brought their pagan rites and paganized the Church

The Roman Church has added popery and many pagan rites and ceremonies that I have pointed out to you. The Reformation of the sixteenth century was a protest against these pagan doctrines and practices and there was a wholesale withdrawal from the Church and a return to the Primitive Church of the New Testament. If the

Roman Catholic Church would renounce popery and these dogmas and practices and hold fast to its primitive foundation, all Christian churches could be united. The term *catholic* applies more to the other churches than to the Roman. Adherence to the gospel of Christ makes a church truly catholic.

CHAPTER X

BAPTISM

ANOTHER of the practices of the church of Rome which cannot be justified in the light of Scripture is the justification of a soul—either infant or adult—through baptism.

Allow me to quote further in proving to you exactly what the Catholic Church teaches; then we shall see what the Scripture says. Here is a quotation from page 18 of "What the Catholic Church Is": "The divinely appointed means of justification is regeneration by water and the Holy Ghost in Baptism. Since justification is a free gift not depending on the act of any creature for its bestowal, even infants can and ought to be baptized. Being baptized, these children are put into the state of justification, and would enter heaven if they die in infancy. On coming to the age of reason, the Church denies the need of any further justification and only requires them to cherish and preserve the grace already possessed by avoiding grievous sin."

"A grown person approaching baptism must do so with faith, sorrow for sin and a desire to receive the grace of the sacrament."

The preceding quotation is the true teaching of Catholicism, which is in constant contradiction to the blessed Word of God. Not one verse of Scripture is given to support these erroneous views. The Scripture has nothing to say about infant baptism, and nowhere in the Bible do we find even a hint that infant baptism saves or cleanses the soul from the original sin of the Adamic nature. I would urge the reader to read, believe and trust in the Word of God before the authority of any church. Romans 5:1 says: "Therefore being justified by faith [not baptism], we have peace with God through our Lord Jesus Christ." Justification is the act of God whereby He declares righteous those who believe in and on the Lord Jesus Christ. This is done without the application of any work on our part. Romans 4:5 says: "But to him that worketh not, but believeth on him that justifieth the ungodly, his faith is counted for righteousness."

To be justified in God's sight is a complete work of grace. The divine act of God by faith in Christ causes us to pass from the realm of sinners to the realm of saints, not because we were baptized, but because we simply believed. If we mortals became Christians through infant baptism, then Christ's sacrificial death was in vain.

Baptism is a symbol—a symbol of what the Holy Spirit did for us the moment we believed on Christ and accepted Him as our personal Saviour. It represents our being buried with Christ and our being raised with Him to newness of life. I believe that every Christian ought to be baptized, by immersion, not for salvation, and not for the purpose of being cleansed from original sin, but as an act of obedience to Christ. Baptism is important in the life of one who has been saved, but it is never essential to salvation, as the Roman Church teaches.

It becomes apparent in the studying and searching of the New Testament Scriptures that baptism was a public and open confession of faith in Christ as Saviour. Studying the method of baptism in the light of the Scripture we find that it requires water: Matthew 3:11; "much water," John 3:23; "down into the water," Acts 8:38; burial in water, Romans 6:4; the resurrection from the water, Romans 6:5. The Greek word for "baptize" is *baptizo*, which means "completely under." Therefore, the proper form of baptism is "immersion."

Many of our Protestant churches practice infant baptism. The greatest mistake of the Reformation was the carrying over of the practice of infant baptism into the new Scriptural movement that was rising against the erroneous teachings and practices of the Church of Rome.

The official Catholic Encyclopedia, sponsored by the Knights of Columbus, with the imprimatur of Cardinal Farley on page 259, volume II, under the heading "Baptism," admits changing the method of baptism. The authors admit that immersion seems to have prevailed until the twelfth century. It has been discovered that Catholic Churches built before the twelfth century possessed the regular baptistry.

I would request the reader to turn to the eighth chapter of Acts, beginning at verse 35. Philip and a eunuch are in conversation about spiritual things. After the eunuch is led to accept Christ as his Saviour, he says to Philip: "What doth hinder me to be baptized? Here is water." Then Philip the Evangelist says, "If thou believest with all thine heart thou mayest." The eunuch answers, "I believe that Jesus Christ is the Son of God."

No man has a right to Christian baptism until he makes this confession that Jesus Christ is the Son of God, and has accepted Him as the Saviour of the world— not only of the world, but of his own individual soul. Now, how can a child, who is but a few weeks old, believe on Christ? How can he confess Christ? Is the child lost because he cannot understand what it means to be a Christian? Now we will look at the entire provision and study the full benefits for all humanity through Christ's death. In I Cor. 15:3 we find that "Christ died for our sins." Therefore, we are delivered from sin through His death. In Romans 5:8 and 9 we find that Christ not only died for us and we are justified by His blood, but we shall be saved from wrath through him." Until a child reaches the age of accountability he is delivered from the sin he inherited by birth, through Christ's finished work. For him the sin question is settled. After he has reached the age of accountability, it is no longer the sin question; it is then the Son question: "What will you do with Jesus?" He is a free moral agent and must decide this question for himself. If he believes on Christ and accepts Him as his Saviour, he escapes condemnation and inherits everlasting life. If he refuses to believe and continues to reject Christ, he shall not have life; the wrath of God abideth on him, and he shall come into condemnation.

Nowhere in the Scripture can we find any authority for justification through baptism, either for children or adults. One must say to any church who leads its people in darkness and ignorance, "Ye do err, not knowing the power of God, nor the scriptures" (Matt. 22:29). Baptism of infants can be traced to heathen practice in the days of Babylon.

The true Church of Christ is invisible, made up of truly converted people who are to be found in all the visible churches and whose names are written in heaven; these visible churches exist to train saints for the kingdom of Christ.

Chapter XI

TWO LETTERS

THE following two letters of June 4 and July 13 have recently been sent to two priests, but to date no replies have come. Each priest received a self-addressed stamped envelope for a reply and was told that after six weeks, if no reply was received, these letters would be published and used as I saw fit for the interest of the kingdom of God.

The purpose of these letters was to gain first-hand knowledge concerning the "reason why" of Catholic teachings, which are contrary to the Word of God. These letters are not meant to stir up antagonism or to offend, but to present Biblical truth in the light of Holy Writ.

I am endeavoring in these two letters to show that it is not what man says or does that is authentic, but what the Bible teaches to be the final analysis of what is truth.

These two letters have been written with much prayer, love and sympathy for the interest of thousands of Roman Catholics who have heard me preach, and scores that have been converted under my humble ministry.

I trust that these two letters will be instrumental in opening the eyes of hundreds who shall read these pages, knowing who is in error and who errs. May the truth of God's Word that is presented in these two letters open your eyes and touch your heart and make you say, "Lord, I believe. Help me always to live in the light of Thy Word, because Thou art Light" (John 8:12; 9:4).

Saturday, June 4, 1938
New Castle, Pa.

Reverend Coyle
St. John's Roman Catholic Church
Fairview, New Jersey
My Dear Rev. Coyle:

Your letter of June 1 received in answer to mine of May 30, in which I asked for information concerning your statement in which you took for a text in your message "And God said, Pray for the dead."

Your answer to my question in reference to the place where this statement was found was that it was found in the second book of the Maccabees, the twelfth chapter and the 46th verse.

I am well aware of the fact that this is one of the Apocryphal books added to the Bible by the Council of Trent in the year 1546 (these books were not recognized as canonical by the Jewish Church). I have been told by other priests that the works of the Apocryphal books are not inspired but were added because of their moral influence. Jesus in His ministry never once referred to quotations from the Apocrypha, but referred always to the *Law*, *Psalms*, and *the Prophets*. Since the Christian Church today is a New Testament Church, I am again taking the liberty of asking you a few questions which you may answer anywhere from the New Testament.

We all know that true Christianity is taught in Holy Writ. It was agreed that the Holy Scriptures are the books of the Old Testament and the writings of the Apostles. One must not forget the books that we now have (not the added Apocryphal) in Old and New Testaments are considered inspired, which I firmly accept and believe. This was universally accepted by the Church Fathers of the fourth century. Thus the Church had its double canon of Scriptures.

Then followed the questions that have been quoted in the letter to Rev. Coughlin.

Wednesday, August 3, 1938
Fairview, New Jersey

Rev. Coughlin
Royal Oak, Michigan
My dear Rev. Coughlin:

As a former member of the Roman Catholic Church, this afternoon I take the liberty in writing you this heart-to-heart letter.

I have been a Roman Catholic for some sixteen years until miraculous Providence led me in the path of studying the Scriptures.

Since reading Holy Writ for the last 12 years, I have found that the Roman Church does not teach or preach the Word of God as she claims, because of the many practices now in the Roman Church which are contradictory to the Word of God and absolutely ridiculous to reason.

I have listened to much of your dogma over the air and much of it appeals to me as being very sound and fundamental; because of this and your wide knowledge in the political field, and due to the fact that you represent fourteen million Roman Catholics in America and I represent ninety-two million Protestants of all denominations in America, I feel that I can come to you as a Christian gentleman in regard to spiritual things.

Be assured that I am writing to you with an open mind and that this is being done for the interest of truth; surely truth can stand opposition and testings and abuse, but it will always prevail.

The following thirty questions can be answered anywhere from the New Testament—either the King James, American Standard, or the Douay Versions—the latter being the version and legitimate authority of the Roman Church. I will not accept the authority of any church, (that includes the Protestant Church as well as the Roman Church) popes, bishops, cardinals, monks, councils, saints, traditions, ministers, laymen, but only THE WORD OF GOD.

I understand that the Roman Catholic Church believes that tradition is of equal value with the Word of God—yet does not your own Bible say in Mark 7:13: *"Making the Word of God of none effect through your tradition which ye have delivered: and many such like things do ye."*

I am sure if you possess truth as you claim to do, you will not resent this letter but will be more than willing to reply to its contents; if this letter shall be ignored, like two recent letters sent to another priest, it shall be published in my forthcoming book, *Out of the Wilderness*, and used in my evangelistic ministry throughout the country.

Just the *Word of God* will be accepted as final in your reply to this letter; not the footnotes of some man but the *Word of Christ* from the *New Testament*, as all believers according to the Scriptures are in the *New Testament Church*.

Yours in the interest of truth,

John Carrara

I. Where, in the New Testament, does Jesus Christ give the Roman Church power or authority, privilege or rights, or distinction over other churches? You claim to be in the true Church, which you teach is built upon Peter, yet the true Church in the Word of God is built upon *Christ.* Read the book of Ephesians.

II. Where, in the New Testament, does Jesus Christ authorize any man to be successor of St. Peter, or to be the "vicar" of Christ, to be "pope," or to exercise the functions or powers claimed by the popes? Where, in the New Testament, does Christ authorize cardinals? Was not the title of pope, or universal bishop, given first to the Bishop of Rome by the wicked Emperor Phocas in the year 610 A. D.?

III. Where, in the New Testament, does Jesus Christ authorize the pope, cardinal, or bishops, or priests, to establish what they call the "confessional," or to hear confession of sin, or to absolve from sin, or forgive sins? Was not this instituted by Pope Innocent III in the Lateran Council in the year 1215 A. D.? Yet the gospel commands us to confess our sins direct to God. Please read Ps. 51:35; Luke 7:48; 15:21; I John 1:8-9.

IV. Where, in the New Testament, does Jesus Christ authorize people to pray to the Virgin Mary or to dead saints? This was done at the Council of Ephesus in the year 431 A. D., when at this council they made her the mother of God, which is contrary to the Scriptures. Please read Rom. 3:10 and Rom. 3:23. Did not the canonization of dead saints begin with John XV in the year 998 A. D.? Are not all Christians saints? Please read from your Bible Rom. 1:7; I Cor. 1:2.

V. Where, in the New Testament, does Jesus Christ authorize the Roman Catholic Mass? This was adopted as a daily celebration in the year 394 A. D. I know that the Mass was developed gradually as a sacrifice and that attendance was made obligatory in the eleventh century. The gospel teaches that the sacrifice of Christ was offered once and for all and is not to be repeated but only commemorated in the Lord's Supper. Please read Heb. 7:27; 9:26-28; also 10:10-14.

VI. Where, in the New Testament, does Jesus Christ authorize the use of holy water, or command to abstain from the use of meats on Friday, or approve the use of images in the church? Holy water mixed with a pinch of salt and blessed by the priests began in the year 850 A. D.

VII. Where, in the New Testament, does Jesus Christ authorize the kissing of dead men's bones for the cure of sickness? While a

Roman Catholic I did this a number of times in the church at Union City, N. J.

VIII. Where, in the New Testament, does Jesus Christ authorize the doctrine of purgatory (as taught only by the Roman Church) where men suffer for their sins, and their loved ones that remain must have Masses said and light candles for them (and pay for them) and have the priest pray for them, so that in due time their souls may depart from this place and go to heaven? Purgatory was first established by Gregory the Great about the year 593 A. D. This was also claimed as a dogma of faith by the Council of Florence in 1439 A. D. Does not the Bible teach us that His blood cleanses from all sin? Please read I John 1:7-9; Acts 10:43; John 5:24; Rom. 8:1.

IX. Where, in the New Testament, does Jesus Christ authorize the priest pray people out of purgatory? Why didn't Jesus speak about purgatory during His ministry? The Early Church and the Church Fathers never believed in this misleading doctrine called purgatory. A converted priest told me that if the Roman Catholic Church would leave out the doctrine of purgatory (where priests pray for the dead) they would have to close down over night.

X. Where, in the New Testament, does Jesus Christ authorize the building of nunneries and monasteries? Why does the Roman Catholic Church refuse the authorities access to nunneries?

XI. Where, in the New Testament, does Jesus Christ authorize the ceremony of the Roman Catholic Church in regard to its young girls who enter the nunneries called "Being Married to Christ"? This is pagan and a very unscriptural practice. Nowhere in the Bible are we told that if we want to work for Jesus in the spreading of His gospel we are to be shut up in buildings and locked in. Surely if they were out among the poor and fallen could they not do a greater work for God in this way?

XII. Where, in the New Testament, does Jesus Christ authorize us to fast on Friday (as taught by the Roman Catholic Church)? I believe in fasting but not on Friday. Where in the Bible is Lent mentioned? Jesus never spoke about Lent—always to the Jew He spoke about the Passover.

I somehow am convinced that these questions cannot be answered in the light of God's word from the New Testament. Are these not repugnant to the teachings of Christ? I have also made a thorough study of ancient religions and one sees that many of the practices of the Roman Church of today have been drawn from ancient heathenism rather than from Christianity. If you are able to find Scriptures in the New Testament in regard to the questions asked I would appreciate it if when you answer this letter you would enclose chapter and verse from the Bible to answer these and following questions.

XIII. Where, in the New Testament, does Jesus Christ authorize the laity to call the priest "Father"? "Call no man your Father upon the earth: for one is your Father which is in heaven" (Matt. 23:9).

XIV. Where, in the New Testament, does Jesus Christ authorize the authority of papal infallibility? Please read Rom. 3:4, 10-23; John 17:11.

XV. Where, in the New Testament, does Jesus Christ authorize the wearing of a piece of brown cloth with the supposed picture of the Virgin Mary and which is supposed to contain supernatural virtue to protect from all dangers those who wear it on their naked skin? This was invented by an English monk named Simon Stock in the year 1286 A. D. Is not this fetishism?

XVI. Where, in the New Testament, does Jesus Christ authorize the doctrine of seven sacraments? I have been able to find only two —Baptism and the Lord's Supper. Please read in your Bible Matt. 28:19-20; 26:26-28. The doctrine of seven sacraments was affirmed in 1439 A. D.

XVII. Where, in the New Testament, does Jesus Christ authorize the doctrine of the Immaculate Conception as taught only by the Romish Church? This was proclaimed by Pope Pius IX in the year 1854 A. D. Does not the gospel state that all men, with the sole exception of Jesus Christ, are sinners? Mary herself needed a Saviour from sin. Please read Rom. 3:23; 5:12; Luke 1:30, 46.

XVIII. Where, in the New Testament, does Jesus Christ authorize His followers to make the sign of the cross? I always did this as a Roman Catholic boy because I was taught it. Is there supernatural protection in making the sign of the cross? I cannot find it anywhere in Holy Writ.

XIX. Where, in the New Testament, does Jesus Christ authorize His followers to hear and sit through a religious service in a tongue unknown to the average layman? Is not the Mass conducted in the Latin tongue? Nowhere in the Scriptures are we told that Jesus or the Apostles conducted Mass. Isn't this another man-made doctrine?

XX. Where, in the Bible, does Jesus Christ authorize the kissing of the pope's feet or ring? Is not this a pagan custom as the feet of emperors were kissed? This was begun, you know, in the year 709 A. D. The Word of God forbids such a practice. Please read Acts 10:25-26; also Rev. 19:10 and 23:9.

XXI. Where, in the New Testament, does Jesus Christ authorize the celibacy of the priesthood? This, you know, was declared and decreed by Pope Hildebrand (Boniface VII) in the year 1079 A. D. Jesus imposed no such rule nor did any of the Apostles. On the contrary, St. Peter was a married man, and St. Paul says that bishops were to have a wife and children. Please read I Tim. 3:2-5 and 12; also Matt. 8:14-15.

XXII. Where, in the New Testament, does Jesus Christ authorize the teaching of nuns in the Roman Catholic Church?

XXIII. Where, in the New Testament, does Jesus Christ authorize the "Rosary" or the prayer beads? This was introduced by Peter the Hermit in the year 1090 A. D. This was copied from Hindoos and Mohammedans. The counting of prayers is a pagan practice and was condemned by Christ. Please read Matt. 6:5-13.

XXIV Where, in the New Testament, does Jesus Christ authorize that we should bless ourselves with *holy water* on entrance to a Roman Catholic Church? Is not this water that we drink? Where in the Bible does it say that water becomes holy because the priest says a few words in an unknown tongue over it?

XXV. Where, in the New Testament, does Jesus Christ authorize the Roman Catholic Church in *Inquisition of Heretics?* He never taught the use of force in the spreading of *His Holy Word.* This, you know, was instituted by the Council of Verona in the year 1184 A. D.

XXVI. Where, in the New Testament, does Jesus Christ authorize the sale of indulgences (commonly regarded as a purchase of forgiveness and a permit to indulge in sin). The Christian religion as taught in the gospels condemns such a traffic, and it was the protest against this traffic that brought on the great God-sent reformation of Protestantism in the sixteenth century.

XXVII. Where, in the New Testament, does Jesus Christ authorize the doctrine of the Roman Catholic Church called *Transubstantiation?* This was instituted by Pope Innocent III in the year 1215 A. D. By this doctrine, the priest pretends to perform a daily miracle by changing the wafer into the body of Christ and then he pretends to eat Him alive in the presence of the people during Mass. The gospel condemns such absurdities, for the *Holy Communion* is a simple memorial of the sacrifice of Christ. The spiritual presence of Christ is implied in the sacrament. Please read Luke 22:19-20; John 6:35; I Cor. 11:26. I believe that I am right in asking this question for the sake of Scriptural truth.